POPE JOHN PAUL II
A WELCOME VISITOR

An appreciation in words and pictures
in celebration of his visit to Britain
May 28-June 2 1982

Text
Jane Bergin

Design
Peter Butler

Editor
Psyche Pirie

Production Editor
Primrose Minney

IPC Magazines gratefully acknowledges advice and
assistance in the preparation of this publication from the
following: in Rome, The Right Reverend Agnellus
Andrew OFM, Vice-President of the Pontifical
Commission for Social Communications, Osservatore
Romano, Don Domenico Valente and the staff of Famiglia
Cristiana; The Most Reverend Derek Worlock,
Archbishop of Liverpool, The Very Reverend Monsignor
George Leonard, personal assistant to His Eminence
Cardinal Basil Hume, Mr. David Murphy, General
Secretary of the Catholic Truth Society; The Reverend
Christopher Hill, Assistant Chaplain to His Grace the
Archbishop of Canterbury; Mr. Juliusz Englert, Mr. Josef
Rusecki and many other members of the Polish community
in this country.

Official coat of arms of Pope John Paul II.

CONTENTS

THE
MOST LIKED MAN

When the Pope comes to Britain at the end of May to begin his six-day visit, he is sure of a rousing welcome from the Catholics of England, Scotland and Wales, who invited him and, from the two hundred and twenty thousand Poles amongst them, an entirely rapturous reception. But the welcome of the Pope promises to spread far wider. Men and women of all faiths and of none have reacted to the news of the visit with genuine interest and pleasure.

Less than four years ago few people in this country had heard of Karol Wojtyla yet today, as Pope John Paul II, he is regarded as a most inspiring leader, looked on with admiration and affection because he so transparently is what everyone would want him to be: a man of courage, love and goodwill. When early last year a national Sunday newspaper published the results of a poll which asked readers to name their Most Liked Man, they announced that votes had gone by an overwhelming majority to the Pope, which must be one of the most unusual accolades he has ever received.

But then he is a most unusual pope. His warmth and openness, his delight in people and his easy natural manner, have completely changed old ideas about what popes are or are likely to do. There was, you may remember, that non-royal wedding. In the past, princes and princesses have occasionally been married in the Vatican chapels as a special privilege and honour. It speaks a great deal for Pope John Paul's informality that a girl in one of the Rome parishes he was visiting didn't hesitate to ask him to celebrate her wedding. With pleasure – why not? he replied. And so a few weeks later a young electrician and a dustman's daughter were married by the Pope. And again, moved to tears by the poverty of the people in a shanty-town in Brazil, on impulse he took off his own gold ring to give to the parish as a personal gesture of his commitment to help.

Many popes have been the sons of poor men and lived simply in their private lives. In Poland Cardinal Wojtyla was said to own four pairs of shoes, half a dozen aged cassocks and not nearly enough shirts. The white robes Pope John Paul wears these days are the traditional uniform of popes and, since they make it easy for people to recognise him, he willingly conforms to custom, although he is happiest in a plain priest's cassock. He meant exactly what he said when speaking to the young people of France: "I've been Pope for nearly two years, and a bishop for twenty, but for me the most important thing is still the fact that I'm a priest".

He is quite unusual in his determination to go on serving as a working priest and somehow contrives to find the time. There was general amazement on Good Friday last year among people waiting in St. Peter's when they realised that one of the many priests on duty hearing confessions was the Pope, a black cloak over his robes. But

"He will lead his people like a brother and open his arms in love to all the world." So wrote a nineteenth-century Polish poet, prophetically, of the man who would become the first Slav pope – John Paul II.

another Polish priest is one of his greatest heroes, the saintly Father Maximilian Kolbe who, to save the life of a married fellow prisoner, voluntarily went to a dreadful death by starvation in an underground cell in Auschwitz. Pope John Paul reveres his memory and has many times prayed in that very cell. Prayer is the core of Pope John Paul's hidden life and in the Polish tradition he has a great devotion to Mary.

Unlike most popes in recent history who were certain of their call to the priesthood from early life and went straight from school to the seminary, Pope John Paul first thought of a career in the theatre. He is a talented writer who has published poetry and is probably the only pope to have made a reputation as a dramatist. His play, *Outside The Jeweller's,* a study of happy marriage and marriage in crisis, has twice been broadcast in England and won the critics' praise for its candid insights into personal relationships and family pressures. There has probably never been a pope who has had so much experience of ordinary everyday life, or who has known and worked and stayed friends with so many people from such different backgrounds.

No one can doubt his brilliant mind. He has distinguished degrees and was for several years a leading professor of ethics. But it is a rare intellectual who has also spent four years as a manual labourer and never lost touch with his old workmates. Until he left Poland to become Pope he held annual reunions with them all, and though he had become a bishop and a cardinal, they felt quite at ease and still called him Karol. And so did his students and all the friends who went with him on ski-ing trips or climbing holidays or canoe expeditions. He has always loved the outdoor life and has a passion for sport. When he became Pope and was asked to decide what time his inauguration ceremony should start, he fixed on an hour that wouldn't clash with an important football match on television. He won many friends with that simple act.

Pope John Paul's ability to speak to so many in their own language has brought

Above: *at a children's audience hands stretch out in welcome and friendship.* Facing page: *hands of happy reunion. The Pope who left his country to serve the world returns to Poland for a few brief and rapturous days.*

him very close to people. He has fluent French, German, Spanish, Italian, several Slav languages, and also Greek and Latin. When he went to the Far East and it was learned that he was to give an address in Japanese, most people expected to applaud the effort but dreaded the results. Pope John Paul took everyone by surprise with a splendidly spoken oration. Tokyo's most important English language daily, *The Japan Times*, commented that his delivery was most impressive and that he had succeeded in putting across his message as no translation could have done. Given at Hiroshima, it was a heartfelt appeal for peace and an end to violence and hatred between nations and between fellow men. The Pope prepares with as much care for all his journeys, so his good English will be even better by the time he arrives.

The Polish people have long believed that one day their nation would produce a great pope. In the middle of the last century the poet Juliusz Slowacki wrote of the first Slav pope who would lead his people as a brother and open his arms in love to the world. When he was still only a young priest, the mother of one of his greatest friends wrote in the margin of her copy of the poem "This Pope will be Karol".

Facing page: *offering a special tenderness for the suffering, the Pope's consoling words at a service for the sick and handicapped bring a radiant response.*
Right: *thousands of people throng St Peter's Square to take part in Palm Sunday Mass.*
Below: *one of his most endearing characteristics is love for, and rapport with, children. This toddler won Pope John Paul's widest smile.*

GROWING UP IN POLAND

Facing page: *Emilia Kaczorowska, twenty-two, a schoolteacher, and junior officer Karol Wojtyla, twenty-six, on their wedding day in the summer of 1905. Their second son, Karol, became Pope John Paul II.*
Inset: *Emilia Wojtyla with her little son who was nicknamed Lolus or Lolek. She died before he was nine.*
Above: *Karol in 1922, a photograph taken to mark his name day, November 4th. The boy and his father were named after St Charles Borromeo, a sixteenth century bishop and cardinal renowned for his selfless life. This day is now a holiday for all Vatican staff.*

Poland in 1920 was a country aflame with the joy of freedom. It was newly restored to its old independence after savage repressions when even the name of Poland was wiped off the map and the country was partitioned between its three powerful neighbours. The people never lost their longing to throw off foreign rule and clung to their pride in their own culture and traditions, even through the darkest periods when they were forbidden to use their own language. Children born in 1920 were the first generation of free Poles for almost a hundred and fifty years.

The birth of a second son on May 18th 1920 was an immense delight to the Wojtylas, who had lost their only daughter four years earlier after just a few months of life. The cramped three-roomed flat where they lived in the small town of Wadowice thirty miles from Cracow was scarcely big enough, since they already had a fourteen year old son, Edmund. But moving somewhere better was out of the question on their small income. A month later, the child was baptised Karol Josef after his father.

Money was short because Karol senior, though an army officer, held only a modest and poorly paid administrative post in the local recruiting office, not a commissioned rank. To bring in a little extra money towards the elder boy's school fees Emilia Wojtyla used to take in dressmaking. The family flat looked on to a dingy, sunless courtyard so Emilia carried her little son round to the garden of a neighbour, elderly now, who vividly remembers the young mother's intense affection for the baby and her habit of saying "you wait and see what a great man my Lolus will be". Karol was always Lolus or Lolek in the family.

Emilia had been a schoolteacher before she married and her husband was a lifelong student of Polish literature and history with ambitions as a writer. So although they were anything but prosperous it was an educated home. Both parents were deeply religious and as soon as he was old enough little Lolek went with his father to daily Mass at the parish church just across the street. When he began at the kindergarten next door to the church Lolek was a lively child, missing his elder brother who had left to go to medical school, and very ready to make friends. His teachers at the primary school soon began to realise that he was very gifted and, by the time he passed on to the high school, it was clear that he was a boy of remarkable talents.

He really excelled at languages, they thought, but seemed to be clever at everything and much too good at imitating his teachers, to the very great amusement of his fellow pupils. His good-natured friendliness and lack of conceit made him very popular but what impressed his schoolmates most of all was that he was so good at sport. Lolek was always ready to play football or go skating, and when

13

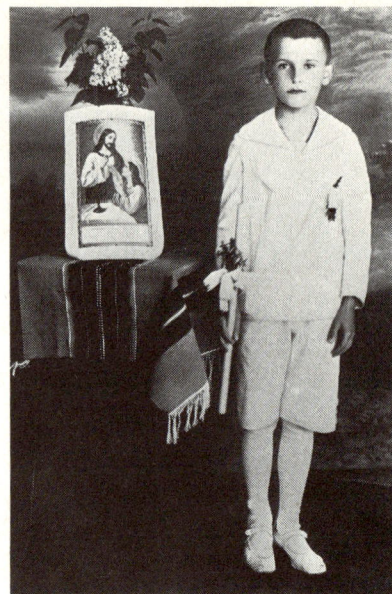

they all took up ski-ing he became known as rather a daredevil. It was a happy time.

His beloved mother's sudden death when he was not yet nine was shattering. Lolek had loved her wholeheartedly and took a long time to regain his carefree cheerfulness. Father and son stayed on in the flat, their life organised to a strict time-table that allowed the boy barely an hour's play before he was summoned to do his homework, always in an unheated room. Karol Wojtyla believed in the value of military discipline and spartan conditions, besides which he couldn't always afford to spend money on heating because Edmund's fees for medical studies had still to be met.

Young Karol was by now very advanced in French, Latin and Greek and turned more and more to the study of literature, declaiming poetry as he raced round the playground with his friends. Then the sudden and tragic death of his brother in an epidemic at the hospital where he had since qualified and was working changed the thirteen year old boy greatly. Though he lost none of his open friendly ways, he became quieter and much more serious. He drew very close to his father and began to devote much of his spare time to keeping him company. Together they walked to many of the shrines to Our Lady that are to be found everywhere in Poland.

As he moved up the high school young Karol's interests deepened. He had always served as one of the altar boys, and now he was their leader. But he also discovered a talent for acting and joined a touring group of schoolboy players in his holidays. The successes he won in the drama festivals pointed the way to a stage career. When he passed his final school examinations with brilliant marks in the summer of 1938, he had already decided to go to the Jagiellonian University in Cracow to take a degree course in Polish language and literature.

Father and son left Wadowice and found themselves in a basement flat in Cracow, within walking distance of the University. It was an even more modest home than before. Karol's father had retired prematurely because of poor health and they now had to manage on a slender pension. But nothing dampened the young man's spirits as he enrolled for literature and philosophy courses and threw himself into student life. After the friendly drabness of Wadowice, he delighted in the beauty of the fourteenth century university, the superb architecture of the city and the famous Wawel that is cathedral and royal castle, the burial place of the kings of Poland and the shrine of the nation's history. He joined a well known experimental drama group, began to write poetry, took part in literary evenings and made hundreds of friends. One vacation he took a job as assistant cook on a building site. At the end of his first year he was one of the university's best-known students.

14

The outbreak of war in September 1939 opened another dark chapter in Poland's tragic history. The Germans stormed in and defeated the small, ill equipped army in a matter of days. An occupation of terrifying severity began. The Poles were treated as a slave people, fit for nothing better than mindless labour. Universities were closed, professors and staff hunted down and imprisoned, and students made forcibly aware that they must abandon all thoughts of education and conform to the will of their conquerors. All had to register for manual work and anyone picked up without papers was instantly deported to a German slave camp.

So began for Karol a strange and secret double life. The strong, well built young man got himself taken on in the stone quarries owned by the Solvay chemical factory a few miles away, and trudged off daily to backbreaking work at the stone face. By night he slipped through the street patrols in defiance of the curfew and the very real risk of being shot on sight, to rendezvous with other students determined to keep the mind and spirit of Polish learning alive. Seminars and lecture courses were held, the flying university moving from house to house with word of the next meeting passed from one to another. Karol did not keep his studies secret from his workmates. Instead he used the lunch breaks to set up an education centre at the factory to encourage others to see themselves as free men of ideas and dignity.

Long, exhausting days at the factory, hours of study at night, combined with

Facing page, far left: Karol when he was at the primary school across the square from his home. In this group of classmates he stands on the left of the back row.
Left: dressed for his First Communion which he made at the parish church were he had been baptised.

Left: the house in Koscielna Street where Karol Wojtyla was born, just off Market Square in Wadowice. The town when Poland was partitioned was ruled by the more liberal Austrians, so had a long tradition of love for the arts and Polish culture.
Above: the Wojtyla family home was on the first floor of the Koscielna apartment block. Their front door opened into the kitchen which was also the living room. Of the two bedrooms, Karol had the one which looked across to the parish church.

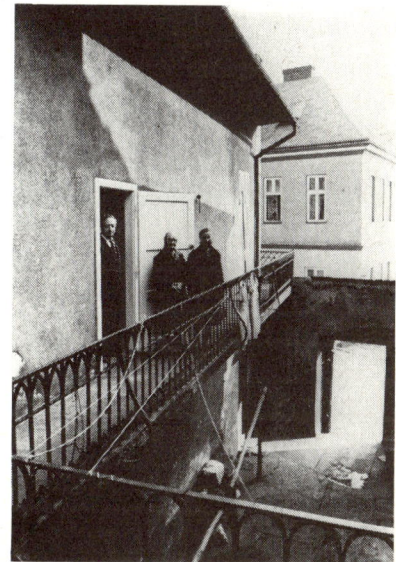

Above: *Karol with his fellow altar boys —*
he is seated second from the left — and the
parish priest who trained them in their
duties. He later became their leader.

caring for his ailing father and trying to exist on the starvation rations that were all
that was allowed the despised Poles, were a desperate strain. Early in 1941 Karol's
spirit was tested to the depths. Returning one day from work after collecting some
medicines for his father and a meal cooked for them by a friend's mother, he entered
the flat and found his father had died of a heart attack. He was devastated with grief
and for twelve hours remained kneeling by his father's body in agonised distress that
the old man should have had to die alone.

Not long before, there had lived with the Wojtylas the young Kotlarczyks,
friends from Wadowice to whom father and son had offered a home when they had
been forced out of their flat. Mietek Kotlarczyk was a passionate enthusiast for the
theatre and he and Karol had set up, in the spirit of cultural resistance, the Rhapsodic
Theatre, a band of actors who gave clandestine performances of patriotic verse
dramas, performed in secret without props or costume and relying for their effect on
the perfection with which every word of the text was spoken. The Rhapsodic Theatre
was Karol's lifeline. So was the Living Rosary, a prayer group organised by a
remarkable layman who earned his living as a tailor and gathered round him a
number of devout young men. Karol in his turn gathered more students and guided
them in their spiritual life.

A serious street accident, when he was knocked down by a lorry and fractured his
skull, put him in hospital for some weeks. He began to wonder if, now that he was
alone in the world with no family responsibilities, he should consider becoming a
priest. But he put the thought aside, feeling he would do best to pursue his studies
and his theatre. Then a second street accident, when he was nearly crushed to death
by a tram, put him in hospital again and again forced him to reflect on the course of
his life. When he returned at last to the factory, well but with a slight stoop as a result
of one shoulder now being higher than the other, he had made up his mind. He
would offer himself for the priesthood.

16

To become a priest in occupied Poland was most dangerous. Seminaries had been closed, every priest was under suspicion and hundreds had been arrested on trumped up charges. More than two thousand were to die in concentration camps. Karol enrolled in the underground theological department that was part of the flying university. For the next two years he continued at the Solvay factory, where he now worked in the shot-firing department thanks to a friendly foreman who got him promoted to a job where he was able to read between his tasks. He went on with his clandestine talks and lectures to his work-mates in the lunch breaks, prayed and talked with his Living Rosary groups, taking them on country walks when the weather was fine and there seemed less risk of German round-ups, and began his programme of studies for ordination.

But even a prodigious worker like Karol had to accept there was a human limit. His acting friends were regretful, but not surprised, when he told them not to cast him for any more parts in the Rhapsodic Theatre.

In 1944 Karol suddenly disappeared from circulation and friends at the factory and in Cracow were concerned. He was reported to the German authorities as an absentee worker and his name placed on the list of wanted men. In fact, with other theological students, he had been summoned into hiding in the Archbishop's Palace in Cracow by the indomitable Archbishop Sapieha who was determined to protect them from the round-ups that were becoming increasingly common.

Life in the huge-roomed, appallingly cold palace was austere even for occupied Poland. The students slept in improvised bunk beds with scanty coverings and food was shorter than ever for fear that the Germans might discover more people were in the palace than had their grudging permission to be there. The young men were bundled into old, discarded cassocks in the hope that, in case of emergency, they would be taken for members of the archbishop's staff. Only in January 1945, when the Russians swept into Cracow, were Karol and his companions able to walk free.

Below left: *Marcin Wadowita High School which Karol attended between the ages of eleven and eighteen. As Cardinal Wojtyla he was guest of honour at the centenary celebrations in 1967.*
Below: *Karol Wojtyla at eighteen, a portrait taken just after he moved to Cracow to enter the Jagiellonian University.*

PRIEST
AND PASTOR

Facing page: *Cardinal Wojtyla on a visit to his Milan publishers from Rome, where he was serving on a Vatican commission. He is the author of five books and more than seventy major essays. He has also written plays and poems.*
Above: *Karol Wojtyla became a bishop at the unusually early age of thirty eight. He was the youngest bishop in Poland and one of the youngest in the world.*

Karol Wojtyla was ordained a priest on November 1st 1946, All Saints Day. The following morning he celebrated his first Masses, in memory of his parents and brother. The old priest who guided him through the ceremony remembers how touched he felt that young Father Karol had no family to be with him on such a happy day. At a reception afterwards his friends were disappointed when he broke the news that, instead of staying in Cracow, he was to be sent abroad. They hoped he might become a chaplain at the Jagiellonian University where he had returned for the last few terms of his studies and had been a popular vice chairman of the student's council. But Archbishop Sapieha wished him to go at once to Rome for two years of higher studies. It was an honour, but it was also an exile.

The archbishop was a farseeing man but he could hardly have realised how important those two years were to be. In Rome the young priest enrolled at the Angelicum University where all the lectures were given in Latin, and soon he was able to speak and write almost effortlessly in the official language of the church, thanks to his old love of the classics. He found lodgings at the French speaking Belgian College where the life of the common room improved his good French to an easy fluency. He was studying the works of the Spanish mystic St John of the Cross and set himself to master Spanish. He picked up Italian almost casually, hearing it all around him as he went about the city.

He wrote constantly to friends in Cracow sending greetings, enquiring about everyone and begging for news. He was homesick for Poland and hoped to return for Christmas, or at least for the summer holidays; but the archbishop asked him to stay abroad and see what he could do to help refugee Poles trying to make new lives in France, Holland and Belgium. Archbishop Sapieha also wanted to know more about the pastoral work being done in the industrial parishes in France. Karol was very impressed with the experiment where a group of priests took a flat in a tenement block and lived in the midst of ordinary families. Such close personal contact and experience of everyday problems strengthened understanding between Church and people, he reported.

In 1948, with a brilliant doctorate to his credit, Karol returned home. Poland was no longer a free country. The elections held the previous year had been manipulated and a regime totally hostile to Christianity was in power. Political parties had been dissolved, public meetings forbidden, hundreds of priests had been arrested, religious education banned from schools, university courses were being reorganised on Marxist principles, and all intellectuals were under suspicion.

The country parish of Niegowic where he was sent to be a village curate was too remote to attract much attention from the authorities and certainly the peasants who lived there never thought of Karol as an intellectual. To them he was the smiling young priest who had arrived on foot carrying his few possessions, who took over labouring jobs when any of the farmhands fell ill, who tramped from hamlet to hamlet if no farmcart was going rather than take anyone away from his work, whose words when he preached were so simple and moving that everyone wanted to hear him. He had such a way with children that more and more wanted to be altar boys, and the girls sewed him a goosefeather quilt – which he asked their permission to give to a poor family. Though he made himself so available, Karol continued studying. He won a second doctorate for a thesis he submitted to his old university and, after scarcely a year, he was recalled to Cracow.

The villagers he had left came in for hard words from the parishioners of St Florian's in Cracow, who were shocked when their new priest arrived driving a rickety old cart with all his worldly goods in one small suitcase. He should have been sent in a taxi, they said, and it was disgraceful that he had so few clothes. They soon came to realise that he was quite indifferent to comfort. According to the parish housekeeper, he hardly used his bed at all but knelt for hours in the unheated church and if he returned to the house he slept on the floor. He wore the same patched

cassock until the outraged faithful clubbed together to buy a replacement and took the precaution of asking the parish priest to order him to accept it.

Though Father Karol obediently wore the cassock, the overcoat they had also provided was never seen on his back. Given to some poor man, the people of St Florian's supposed, mildly irritated but not at all surprised. Anyone could come to see him at any time, with any kind of problem. He visited every home, knew all the families and seemed to know most of the university students as well. Students were in and out of the house at all hours and crowded St Florian's every time he preached.

But Father Karol, remembering his own factory days, was just as interested in the young working people who were experiencing the problems of living in a system where an active faith was discouraged and an unthinking conformity dinned in by slogans. His deep concern was to awaken people's minds and though his sermons on Christian ethics were long, they were too short for his younger listeners. To organise meetings except in church without attracting unwelcome attention from the state was difficult, so discussions continued under the guise of sporting activities.

He would get up a party for a ski-ing trip, say Mass for his young friends up in the mountains and spend the evening talking and singing in a mountaineer's hut before

Far left: *picnic on the banks of a lake.*
Karol chats with another professor, his close
friend Jurek. Karol, Jurek and his wife
had many discussions on the theme of
marriage and family life.
Left: *as a young priest in Cracow in his late*
twenties.
Below: *in short-sleeved open neck shirt,*
wearing sunglasses, Karol rounds the bend
of a river. Behind him is the student friend
who taught him how to handle a kayak.
Karol's canoe expeditions on the Masurian
lakes generally lasted a fortnight.

returning home. In the summer they often bicycled out into the country, and the students who sometimes called him Uncle in affectionate deference to his thirty years, but more often Karolek, learned to keep an eye on his erratic progress and shout warnings. He was apt to run into trees or wobble into ditches when he was seized by an interesting train of thought. Hiking presented fewer problems, and he was skilful at handling a canoe on the much loved Masurian lakes.

The church authorities urged him to embark on an academic career. It meant leaving St Florian's and giving up day-to-day parish work. Although he was posted to the other side of Cracow to study and qualify to teach at university level, most of his old parishioners managed to drop in at the two-roomed flat he shared with his supervising professor, and they asked him back for marriages and christenings.

He was invited to lecture at the independent University of Lublin in eastern Poland, which the government could not close because they did not hold its purse-strings. His lectures, invariably crowded, were notorious for never beginning on time; but this was easily forgiven. He was, after all, commuting two hundred miles by overnight train. Soon he was made Professor of Ethics, and for the first time had a salary coming in, and just as rapidly going out as he donated almost all of it, quite anonymously, to needy students. He had been told to give up pastoral duties,

Above: *Cardinal Wojtyla at Kasprowy
Wierch, the highest peak in the Tatra
mountains close to the Czechoslovak border.
He was once held in custody for several hours
for crossing accidentally, as the police
refused to believe his identity papers. A skier
of near championship standard, he loved
tackling the most dangerous ski runs.*
Above right: *shaving in a forest glade.
Bishop Wojtyla on a camping trip in the
mountains in 1959.*

but nothing had been said about pastoral pleasures. So he felt free to continue his contacts with the young students and workers of Cracow, and the weekend expeditions went on as cheerfully as before.

He was miles away leading a party canoeing on the Masurian lakes when he was tracked down and summoned to see Cardinal Wyszynski in Warsaw and given the news that he was to be made a bishop. It was a surprise appointment and at his request not made known until he had returned to his friends to finish the planned trip, ending as usual with Mass on the banks of a lake, two paddles lashed together to do duty as a cross. At thirty eight he was much the youngest bishop in Poland.

Wawel Cathedral was thronged the day Karol was consecrated as bishop, to be assistant to the Archbishop of Cracow. Childhood friends travelled from Wadowice, highland people came down from the mountains, there were farming families from his first country parish, all the students he had grown up with, old workmates from the Solvay factory, a huge contingent from St Florian's, colleagues from Lublin University, friends from the Living Rosary circle, actors, writers, journalists, hundreds of young people.

He was determined that nothing should seem to distance him. He continued, against much advice, to live in his little flat and persuaded the archbishop to let him carry on as a working professor in Lublin. He was reluctant to abandon anything. When he fell ill and was confined to bed for some weeks, critics said he had been asking for trouble. His illness was a blood disorder, similar to a mild form of leukaemia. He was delighted when his doctor told him that the best way to recover his health and prevent further attacks was strenuous exercise, preferably in the open air. Never was a patient more ready to follow medical advice to the letter. He took it as an indication that his constitution thrived on work, and put into operation a plan that widened his contacts further.

He began to invite groups of all kinds to his flat for informal evenings of discussion – scientists, doctors, lawyers, writers – everyone who enjoyed exchanging ideas. His invitations were eagerly accepted. Marxists were welcomed, for he wanted to know people of all shades of opinion. Everybody felt at ease and the evenings generally

Left: *dressed in the knickerbockers he preferred for cycling, Karol stands smiling in the sun. After a serious illness he made a habit of cycling every day.*
Above: *the Archbishop of Cracow at his most informal, in weatherproof jacket and running shoes, carrying a loaded rucksack. On walking trips in the mountains the party carried all the provisions they would need for their journey. Karol also carried his Mass vestments.*

ended with singing traditional folk songs, the bishop leading and playing the guitar.

Though political pressures had been increasing, and the primate of Poland, Cardinal Wyszynski, had been placed under house arrest for three years, Karol had not clashed with the authorities. But inevitably as a bishop he had to challenge them. He did so firmly, patiently and quite implacably at Nowa Huta, the steel town that had been built on the outskirts of Cracow. Nowa Huta was a great industrial centre, a town for modern communist man and therefore a town without God. Factories, workers' flats, schools, shops but no church, although the thousands who lived there petitioned again and again for a site. Permission was reluctantly granted during a period of temporary relaxation and then abruptly withdrawn.

Insistently Bishop Karol pressed the case, giving the authorities no peace over nine years, rallying support from friends abroad, raising funds and celebrating Mass year after year on the empty site until in 1967 the state gave way. It took the people of Nowa Huta another ten years before their much-desired church was ready. They built it with their own hands, a spectacular church in the shape of a great ship sailing in the sky above the squalor of the town.

There were other victories. When one of his priests reported that he had incurred a huge fine and the alternative was a prison sentence, Karol told him to report to the

Above: *the famous church at Nowa Huta, consecrated by Cardinal Wojtyla on May 15th 1977. He used to celebrate open-air Mass on the site for years before the authorities allowed building to begin.*
Left: *the smiling Cardinal Wojtyla answers a journalist's question. His lively personality and ready wit made him a great favourite with the overseas press.*
Right centre: *the Archbishop of Cracow magnificently vested for a great ceremonial occasion in the cloth of gold chasuble dating from the sixteenth centruy. The ornate jewelled crozier has belonged to the cathedral since the time of King John III Sobieski, who saved Vienna from the Turks in 1683.*
Below: *Cardinal Wojtyla abroad. In the years before he became Pope he visited north and south America, Australia and the Pacific islands to represent the Polish bishops at congresses and international gatherings.*
Far right: *Cardinal Wyszynski (left) and Cardinal Wojtyla en route to Rome for the August conclave in the year of three popes.*

prison at once. The diocese had no funds for fines. He went himself to the parish, took all the Sunday services and at each one explained from the pulpit for the benefit of the secret police taking notes at the door that he would personally act as parish priest as long as the prison sentence lasted. The authorities backed down, released the imprisoned priest in a matter of days, and nothing more was heard of the fine. The bishop returned to Cracow and also let matters rest. He did not believe in rubbing in a triumph.

As one of sixteen Polish bishops, led by Cardinal Wyszynski, he went to Rome in 1962 to attend the first meeting of the Vatican Council, when bishops from all over the world were called together by Pope John XXIII to discuss every aspect of the Church's life and mission. Bishop Karol made a great impression on the gathering for his open approach, lively interest in every issue and his winning personality. His gift for languages was a tremendous asset in exchanging ideas and striking up friendships.

The debates at that first meeting of the council were held in Latin and Karol's ability to speak it so fluently, and the clarity and power of his contributions, were widely admired. He was a passionate supporter of a declaration on liberty of conscience for all men. Inspired by the sense of common purpose and dedication that he found

Left: *as a young bishop attending the Vatican Council, Karol shows his old friend Mietek the glories of St Peter's. Mietek Kotlarczyk and his wife shared the Wojtylas' flat for a time, and the two young men started the Rhapsodic Theatre. Mietek became a well known theatre director. Karol wrote his poem 'Marble Floor', inspired by St Peter's.*

Above right: *no Polish celebration is complete without flowers, though generally they are presented more ceremoniously. To laughter all round, the smiling cardinal takes aim with one of the flowers tossed at him during a feast-day party.*
Above: *the very small, simply furnished bedroom that Karol Wojtyla used when he moved into the Archbishop's Palace in Cracow. He kept only three rooms for his own use in the vast building.*

amongst his fellow bishops, he wrote some of his most moving poems at this time.

When he was appointed Archbishop of Cracow and became head of the diocese, he reluctantly moved from his flat to the Archbishop's Palace, where many years before he had been in hiding as a student priest. He kept only three rooms in the vast building for himself. One wing he turned into a rest home for the chronic sick. Each morning he set aside two hours when anyone who wanted his help could come off the street to see him, and his waiting room was always crowded. He was endlessly patient in listening to the little worries that so concern old people, but many of the problems brought to him were very serious – harassment by the police, marriage difficulties, unemployment, bad housing. He set up a family centre, headed by a woman psychiatrist with doctors, priests and lawyers on hand to give further help. Every evening there were meetings, conferences, groups and gatherings he had initiated taking place all over the palace. He visited them all and seemed to work very nearly a twenty-four hour day.

Though he was made a cardinal in 1967 it made little difference to his Cracow lifestyle. Instead of a cardinal's scarlet he continued to wear his plain black cassock, walked about the city from parish to parish, stopping dozens of times on the way as he caught sight of anyone he had met in the past to ask warmly after their concerns, recalling incidents and details of conversations that had taken place years ago. As the second cardinal in Poland, and loyal assistant to the indomitable Cardinal Wyszynski, he now had duties beyond his diocese, so he needed a car. To his friends' sighs of relief, he decided not to waste time driving it himself, but had a reading light and desk installed so he could go on working while he was on the move.

He was also serving on several important commissions at the Council in Rome where his abilities and his complete lack of vanity won him great respect. He would listen very reflectively and intently to all the views others expressed and never urged his own claims to speak, quite content to wait till last. How fortunate that he was such an unassuming man, one of the bishops said thoughtfully, because whenever he joined in the debates he spoke so compellingly and wisely that there was seldom anything to add.

He travelled widely to represent the Polish bishops at congresses and conferences in Europe, the Americas and Australia, lectured in philosophy to great acclaim at a summer school at Harvard, published scholarly papers, addressed learned gatherings. In the highest circles of the church he was becoming known as a man of rare gifts and spirituality, with a radiant personality that impressed everyone he met. But at home in Cracow he was simply Karolek, loved for his goodness and everyone's friend.

EX ORDINE PRESBYTERORVM
EX ORDINE PRESBYTERORVM
EX ORDINE PRESBYTERORVM
EX ORDINE DIACONORVM

THE NEW POPE

Facing page: *members of the College of Cardinals at the special Mass held to pray for wisdom and enlightenment before they enter the conclave.*
Above: *Cardinal Basil Hume during the Mass before conclave that was to elect Pope John Paul II. He was regarded as a possible choice for the office.*

White smoke was seen pouring, on the evening of Monday October 16th 1978, from the chimney above the Vatican's Sistine Chapel where the conclave of cardinals had met two days earlier. A decision had been reached and a new pope elected. Twenty minutes later came the official announcement, made by Cardinal Felici in the Latin that the Catholic Church still uses on its most solemn ceremonial occasions and which for seconds, until the meaning was understood, concealed the drama of what he was about to say. "I announce to you a great joy. We have a Pope, the most eminent and reverend lord Karol Wojtyla, Cardinal of the Holy Roman Church, who has chosen the name of John Paul II." It was sensational news in a year of sensations for the Church, the year of three popes.

Pope John Paul is so well known today that it is hard to recapture the shock and amazement that the news of his election caused throughout the world; and not least to the authorities in Poland. They faced not only the unexpected but the virtually unthinkable – yet at the same time, as fellow Poles, they felt a certain horrified pride that one of their countrymen should have been chosen for this unique office.

Two months earlier, on August 6th 1978, Pope Paul VI had died at Castelgandolfo, the small palace in the country outside Rome where popes spend the summer months to escape the heat of the city. He had been in his eighty-first year and seemed older, painfully crippled with arthritis for many months and frail with the worries and turbulence that had beset the Church during his period of office. The cardinals of the world were summoned to Rome to attend the simple funeral he had asked for in his will, and to meet in secret conclave to elect a successor.

Pope Paul had appointed many new cardinals and also ruled that those who had reached the age of eighty should not take part in the voting. One hundred and eleven cardinals entered the August conclave, eleven from north America, nineteen from Latin America, thirteen from Asian countries, twelve Africans and fifty six Europeans, twenty seven of them from Italy. Pope Paul had paved the way, should the cardinals wish, for a pope to come from anywhere in the world. But no one quite believed it would happen, as it did not. Within a single day, only a third of the time taken by most twentieth century conclaves, the cardinals had elected, almost by acclamation it seemed, a gentle smiling Venetian, Cardinal Albino Luciani, who took the unusual double name of John Paul I.

It was a sign of love and respect for Pope John XXIII, who had called the Vatican Council and set in motion all the changes it had brought about – in liturgy, attitudes and the search for Christian unity; and equally in homage to Pope Paul VI, who had tirelessly carried on the Council's work. In retrospect, it is strange that the Venetian pope, when he was asked, according to custom, by what name he wished to be known, should have answered John Paul I. It was almost as if he sensed that there would soon be a second John Paul.

The Venetian pope held office for only thirty-three days, long enough to decline the pomp of a coronation and to ask instead for an installation on the steps of St Peter's, where he spoke with strong feeling of his longing for Christian unity. Less than four weeks later, the world was startled to hear of his sudden death from a massive heart attack. He was genuinely mourned, for he seemed a symbol of gentleness and hope that would be hard to replace.

Once again the cardinals were summoned to Rome, saddened and discouraged but better acquainted with each other and with the procedures. Cardinal Hume flew in from London, uncomfortable in the knowledge that *The Times* had come out with an enthusiastic leading article supporting his claims, claims he would be the last to make, and that *The Guardian* had gone even further and written that he was the favourite to succeed. Cardinal Wyszynski, with Cardinal Wojtyla in his customary place a few respectful steps behind, flew in from Poland to little comment.

The press photographers were taking pictures of all the arrivals at Rome airport, but Cardinal Wojtyla waved them away with the smiling remark that there was no need to take his picture as no one was likely to elect him. A Dutchman, Cardinal Willebrands, was thought to be a probable, and several Italian cardinals were highly regarded. Though in the August conclave ony eleven cardinals had had previous experience of taking part in a papal election, this time they had all been through the elaborate process and knew the thinking that had gone before.

The proceedings of a conclave are secret, and all cardinals take a solemn oath to reveal nothing of how a decision is reached. The only clue for outsiders is the smoke that issues from the Sistine Chapel chimney as, after voting, the ballot papers are destroyed by fire – with the addition of chemicals that will turn the smoke black if the voting has been inconclusive. The voting papers alone should give off the white smoke that is the first sign the conclave has agreed on its choice; but in the past there has been so much confusion about the signals that nowadays chemicals are added.

To be elected, a candidate must receive two thirds of all votes plus one. In rare cases, when there is one outstanding choice, the cardinals can dispense with written

Below: *watching crowds in St Peter's Square turn away in disappointment as black smoke is seen rising from the narrow chimney above the Sistine Chapel. The clock on the façade of the basilica shows twelve noon exactly.*
Below right: *the stove, specially installed in the Sistine Chapel, in which ballot forms are burned to preserve the secrecy of voting. On the right a container holds sticks of chemicals that will produce black or white smoke to signal whether or not a new pope has been elected.*

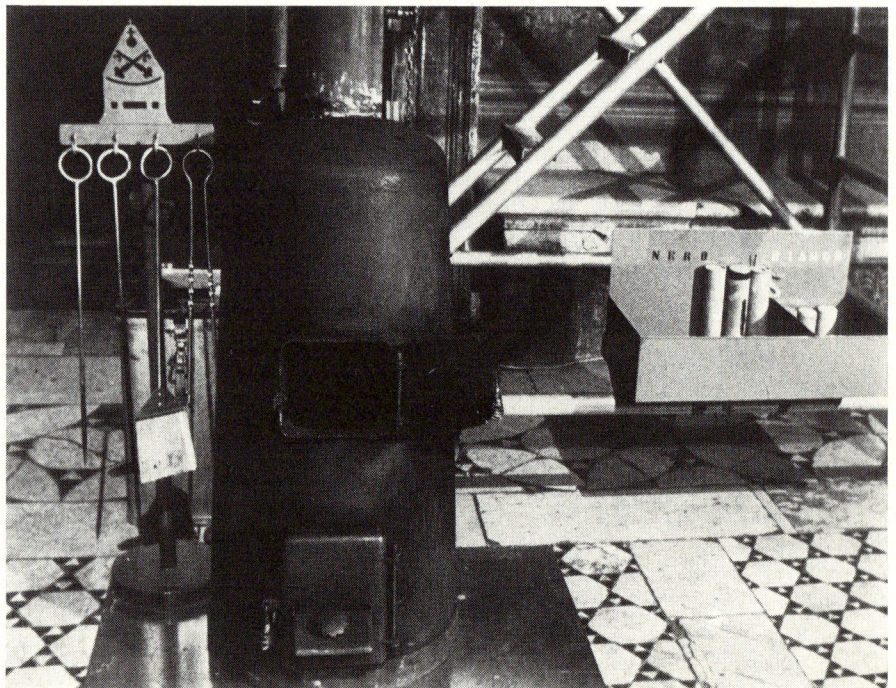

votes and choose by acclamation, though afterwards the choice must be confirmed by everyone individually. They can, if they wish, nominate a select committee of any uneven number between nine and fifteen to do the choosing for them. Though hints are dropped and stories told, no one ever really knowns what takes place behind the locked doors.

But on the following morning, a few seconds before midday, black smoke was observed. The huge Sunday crowd waiting in St Peter's Square was unsurprised but rather disappointed when, in the early evening, black smoke was seen again, whether from one ballot or two, no one can say. The one-day conclave that had elected the Venetian pope was not to be repeated.

Throughout the following day, a working Monday, the crowds thinned and there were many fewer people in the Square. But thousands returned by early evening, and they were not disappointed. Just before twenty minutes past six white smoke was clearly seen and the excitement was great. The Catholic Church feels orphaned without a leader and a new pope is sure of a welcome. As the news of the choice spread through the city thousands more Romans hurried to St Peter's and stood expectantly shoulder to shoulder under a golden harvest moon to see him for themselves. All Catholics, in particular Italians, know of the heroic struggles the Poles have made to keep their religious tradition.

The Pope from Poland, when he appeared on the balcony just before half past seven, was given a delirious reception. Introduced to the people, he was expected to respond to the crowd with a blessing, acknowledge their thanks and withdraw. But

this Pope was to prove himself different. As the crowd shouted their cheers, he moved briskly forward, gripped the balcony in his strong hands and spoke to the people, unrestrained by the whispered advice that only a blessing was customary.

"Praised be Jesus Christ," he said in Italian, and the Roman crowd thought it a graceful courtesy for him to use a traditional Italian greeting and gave the traditional reply "Now and forever". But he went on in good Italian: "Dear brothers and sisters, we are all still grieved at the death of our dear Pope John Paul I and so the cardinals have called for a new bishop of Rome. They have called him from a far distant land – far away and yet always close because of our unity in faith and Christian tradition. I was afraid to accept that responsibility, but I do so in the spirit of obedience to the Lord."

He added a reference to his devotion to Mary, begged them to correct his faulty Italian and ended: "I begin with the help of God and the help of men". When at last he gave the customary blessing to the city and the world, and left the balcony to tumultuous cheers, everyone who had heard him was on his side.

He was the first non-Italian pope for four hundred and fifty years, the first Slav, the first from a country behind the Iron Curtain, the first pope who had lived all his priestly life under communism, the youngest pope, at fifty-eight, for more than a hundred and thirty years – and a pope who was evidently his own man, unafraid to stamp his personality on the papacy from the very first moment.

During the next few days, instead of staying in seclusion, he drove out from the

Left: *breaking all protocol the new Pope spoke directly to the people. The warmth of his charismatic personality was evident from the very start.*
Below: *the most touching moment of the inauguration ceremony. Cardinal Wyszynski, the heroic Primate of Poland humbly kneels to make his obedience to the new Pope who was for so long his loyal assistant.*

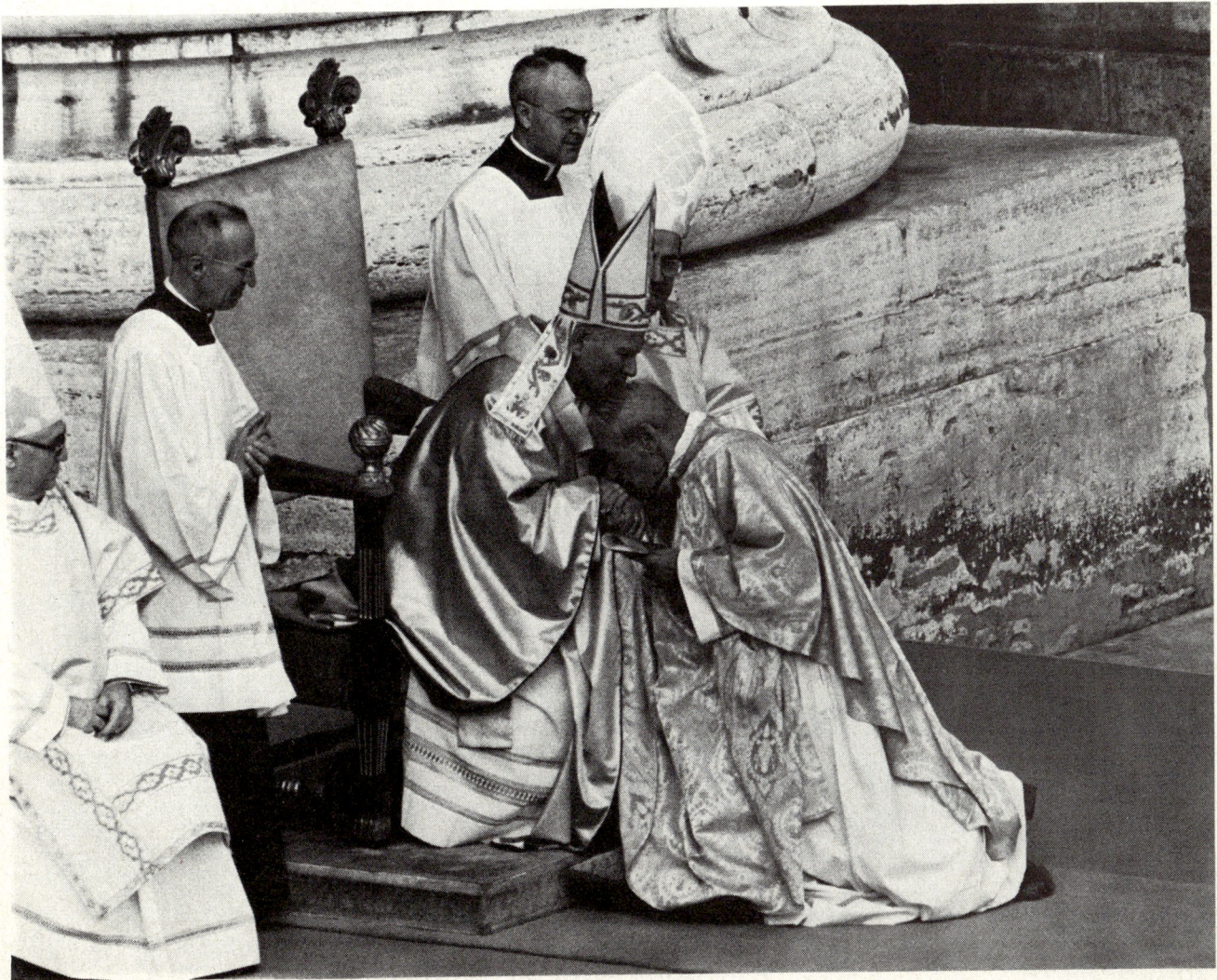

Facing page: *against all precedent the new pope moves down among the crowds after his inauguration Mass.*
Left: *Pope John Paul kneels in prayer at the mountain top sanctuary of Mentorella. He had spent many hours in meditation there before he was elected.*

Vatican to visit an old friend in hospital and greatly pleased people who had gathered outside by his unaffected candour when, reminded by one of the Vatican staff who had accompanied him that he ought to give a blessing he did so, then remarked for all to hear: "There you are, as you can see, even a pope must learn his trade". It was a new perspective on the papacy.

The following Sunday, Pope John Paul II held his inaugural Mass on the steps outside St Peter's in front of thousands of invited guests, and hundreds of thousands more who filled the Square. The Mass was televised throughout the world, and followed with particular fascination in Poland where once again he had gently compelled the authorities to rethink their plans.

For decades the Polish bishops had alternately pleaded and demanded access to the media without avail. Permission for even a broadcast Mass for the benefit of the sick and housebound had never been conceded, and the televising of a religious service was a ludicrous improbability. But a pope from Poland could not be ignored and the inauguration ceremony was shown in its entirety; and everyone living in Poland had the extra pleasure of observing that the communist president, Henryk Jablonski,

35

had felt unable to be absent when other heads of state were there to honour his countryman and was duly seated near the altar.

The intensity of Pope John Paul's concentration at the Mass itself, his submissively lowered head as the yoke of office, the pallium, was placed on his shoulders and his delight and brotherly welcome as the hundred and nine cardinals came forward to promise obedience and were warmly greeted, chatted to and heartily embraced, showed a man of deep faith and ardent charity. In his address he spoke of his sense of unworthiness to succeed to the see of Peter, his unwillingness to accept any symbol of office that might seem to represent claims to pomp or power, his commitment to the service of all mankind – and most movingly to his fellow countrymen of the impossibility of putting into words the feelings of his heart.

He spoke in many languages to all who would hear him. In English he said: "To all

Below: *the Pope's first outdoor audience – before sixty thousand pilgrims who packed St Peter's Square. His specially built car replaced the papal throne on which former popes had been carried.*
Right: *at the Easter ceremonies. Pope John Paul watches the lighting of the first candles that symbolise the joy of the Resurrection.*

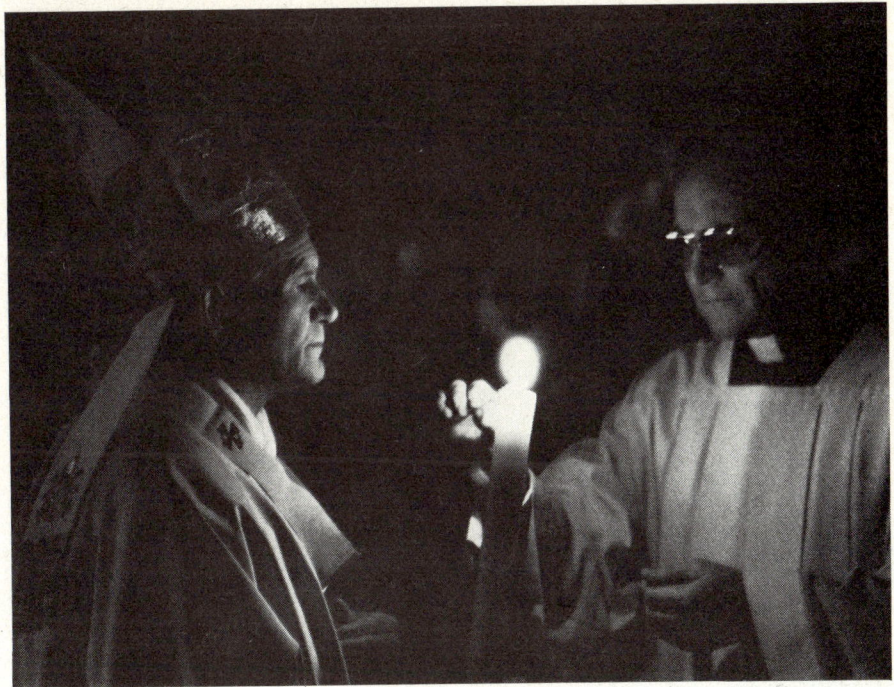

of you who speak English I offer in the name of Christ a cordial greeting. I count on the support of your prayers and your good will in carrying out my mission of service to the Church and to mankind. May Christ give you his grace and peace, overturning the barriers of division and making all things one in him". He spoke in similar terms in French, German, Spanish, Portuguese, Czechoslovakian, Russian, Ukrainian and Lithuanian and he ended with an appeal: "And I also appeal to all men, to every man, to pray for me. Help me to be able to serve you".

The solemn ceremony was over. Karol Wojtyla was Pope John Paul II – and immediately the changes began. Instead of withdrawing with the cardinals in ritual procession he seized his bishop's staff and strode down to move among the crowd, greeting old friends and new, speaking with particular affection and concern to the invalids whose wheelchairs were drawn up in front of the crush barriers, happily waving and smiling in response to ecstatic greetings from the huge Polish contingent that had rushed from all corners of the world to be present.

When at length he left it was to reappear, minutes later, at the balcony of his private apartments and invite the crowd to say the Angelus prayers with him. Afterwards he waved and smiled to resounding cheers, and then said in an agreeably matter of fact way that it was quite time to go home as they all of them, himself included, ought to be eating their lunch. It was a splendidly informal ending to the dignity and emotion of the morning.

Later that same day Pope John Paul held a reception in his private library for Christians from other communions who had attended his inauguration. Dr Donald Coggan, then Archbishop of Canterbury, was amongst them, and so was the Moderator of the Church of Scotland, Dr Brodie, and a large group representing the Methodist Church. The Pope asked them all to join hands as a sign of the mutual wish for unity and said, with great emphasis, "Much has already been done, but we must not stop until we achieve the aim of bringing about that unity of the whole Church for which Christ prayed." He then gave all of them a cheerful and encouraging hug, which most found very exhilarating once they had got over the surprise. Pope John Paul has said that he wishes his to be a ministry of love, and to show the joy of faith to a troubled world. His first days as Pope were convincing proof of his sincerity and a heartening beginning to a new era.

VATICAN VISITORS

Every day when he is in residence at the Vatican, Pope John Paul is at home to a stream of guests, all of whom he receives with a warmth and cordiality that turns even the most protocol-laden meeting into a personal encounter. The official pictures taken on these occasions show beyond doubt how much he enjoys taking every opportunity to make contact, and that he is able to evoke a response of equal pleasure in the people who come to see him.

One of the red-letter days in his crowded engagement diary was October 17th 1980, when Her Majesty the Queen made the most formal of all visits, that of a head of state. Accompanied by Prince Philip and with a large entourage that included the Foreign Secretary, Lord Carrington and Mr Mark Evelyn Heath, then Her Majesty's Minister to the Holy See, the Queen arrived in style. As she was driven along the processional way that leads to St Peter's, thousands of Italians lined the route and waved Union Jacks as they shouted with enthusiasm and commented admiringly on the Queen's elegant appearance. As protocol requires on such occasions, she was dressed in black from head to foot, though all the public could see was her fine black silk veil held in place by a pearl and diamond tiara.

After the procession of cars had swept in through the Arch of the Bells, the official grand entrance to the Vatican to the left of St Peter's Basilica, the Queen was ceremonially received and conducted to the private library where Pope John Paul stood smiling in the doorway waiting to receive her. The Queen was no stranger there. She first visited the Vatican in 1951, in the time of Pope Pius XII, and ten years later went as Head of State to visit Pope John XXIII. On both those occasions the meeting was in the private library, the traditional place for receiving statesmen, diplomats and heads of state. It is a worthy setting to honour important Vatican guests. The beautiful floor is chequered in grey, green and ivory marble, a handsome coffered ceiling with panels decorated in coral and gold rises above a frieze painted with pastoral scenes, and sixteenth-century bookcases filled with rare and valuable editions of the Bible line the walls.

From the first moment when, after a deep bow, Pope John Paul clasped the Queen's hand in his characteristic double grip, the two heads of state made a mutually good impression. Certainly the Pope had been eagerly looking forward to the meeting and wanted to convey not only his personal respect but also his sincere regard for all that the Queen represents. He said as much in his address of welcome: "In the person of Your Majesty I render homage to the Christian history of your people as well as to their cultural achievements. The ideals of democracy, anchored in your past, remain challenges for every generation of upright citizens in

Right: *Pope John Paul bows in deep respect as he greets the Queen on the occasion of her State Visit in October 1980. In her speech the Queen expressed her pleasure that the Pope was to pay a pastoral visit to her Catholic subjects in 1982.*
Overleaf: *the Queen's eyes light up with laughter as Prince Philip jokes with the Pope. Their private conversation overran its scheduled time by fifteen minutes.*

Left: *thoroughly at home after the official speeches, the Queen and the Pope chat together like old friends. The Foreign Secretary, Lord Carrington and Prince Philip also enjoyed this audience in the private library.*

Below left: *the Queen was conducted through the Vatican Palace by Monsignor Jacques Martin, Prefect of the Pontifical Household. Swiss Guards in full ceremonial uniform lined her route. Wearing black according to custom, the Queen chose a full skirted dress of taffeta and velvet.*

Right: *a few weeks after the royal visit Pope John Paul was host to Mrs Margaret Thatcher, who was in Rome for talks with the Italian government.*

your land. In this century your people have repeatedly endeavoured to defend these ideals against aggression. It is my prayer that these great benefits will be effectively guaranteed for future generations."

He went on to speak of his deep satisfaction at "the zeal with which representatives of the Catholic Church and the Anglican Communion have pursued the noble goal of drawing closer together in Christian unity and in effective common service to humanity" and added that he looked forward with great anticipation to making a pastoral visit to the Catholics of Great Britain "both as sons and daughters of the Catholic Church and as loyal citizens of the nation".

The Queen spoke as warmly in reply, referring to the growing cordiality of the welcome extended over the years to members of the royal family and saying, "We in turn welcome the visit Your Holiness is planning to pay in 1982 to the Roman Catholic community in Great Britain . . . we support the growing movement of unity between the Christian churches of the world and we pray that Your Holiness's visit to Britain may enable us all to see more clearly those truths which both unite and divide us in a new and constructive light." The Queen ended by wishing the Pope strength and inspiration in the great task to which he was committed.

After the formal speeches and introductions of accompanying officials, Pope John Paul had a private talk with the Queen and Prince Philip, scheduled to last for twenty five minutes. Their informal chat continued for forty minutes and all three were beaming when they came to make the exchange of gifts with which all such visits customarily conclude. The Pope's gift to the Queen was one of the treasures of the Vatican library, a rare illuminated edition of Dante.

The Queen's visit, which took place on a Friday, the day when heads of state are generally received, had been the highlight of another busy week. Pope John Paul had seen cardinals and bishops from Mexico, Colombia and Peru on the Monday, the Patriarch of Antioch and accompanying prelates of the Greek rite on Tuesday

Top: *invited to Rome by the Italian labour movement in January 1981, five months after the signing of the Gdansk agreement that won the Poles the right to organise free trade unions, Solidarity leader Lech Walesa thanks the Pope for giving Polish workers courage and hope.*

Top right: *West German Chancellor Helmut Schmidt is welcomed by the Pope who paid an extensive visit to Germany some months later.*

Above: *almost his first visitors were King Juan Carlos and Queen Sophia of Spain. By historic privilege Queens of Spain may wear white at papal ceremonies.*

Above right: *King Hussein of Jordan called on Pope John Paul during a tour of European countries. The Pope favours international status for Jerusalem.*

morning, North American archbishops of the Ukrainan rite the same afternoon, West African, South African and Sudanese archbishops and bishops the next day, and several archbishops from the United States on Thursday morning. As members of the family they were received with little formality, as are cardinals and archbishops who head important departments in the church's organisation in Rome and have regular appointments. They come and go, as often as not on foot, through the Porta Sant' Anna, the workaday entrance to the Vatican.

Through this gateway, a couple of hundred yards to the right of St Peter's Square, the public may pass without prior permission to reach the offices of the Vatican newspaper. This is a popular destination after every public audience as the photographs taken can be inspected and souvenir copies obtained. The vigilant Swiss Guards, in the less colourful white-collared navy blue uniforms they wear when not on ceremonial duty, make discreetly certain that these callers do not stray further than the newspaper office. Even so, there is often the opportunity to see troops of bishops leaving after they have been to see the Pope, since one of the lifts from his apartments descends on this side of Vatican Palace.

In the week the Queen came to see him, Pope John Paul received the President of Mali and his suite in private audience. Many countries have ministers or ambassadors accredited to the Vatican and newly independent Third World states are no

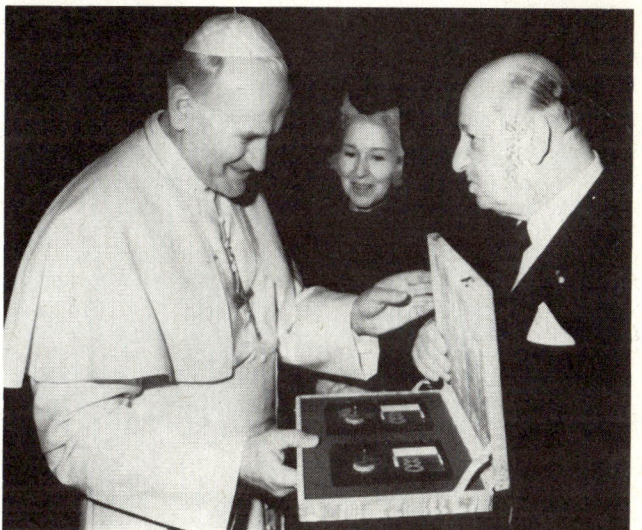

exception. Whatever the political views of their governments, they value these contacts highly because they are all aware how much missionary, educational and welfare work the Church undertakes.

Pope John Paul is glad to give his support and encouragement to all who are prepared to stand up and speak out for high standards. Royalty, trade unionists, scientists, artists, authors, doctors, economists and many others of all nations ask to see the Pope and talk to him about their lives and their work, and often to ask his blessing. Statesmen and politicians regard a call on the Pope as a valuable opportunity to talk over social and political principles and be aware of his particular spiritual insights. All respect his advocacy of human rights and commitment to peace and his willingness to take initiatives that will promote dialogue.

These conversations are, of course, confidential and remain unrecorded but it is known that the Pope does not confine himself to vague generalities. He takes the opportunity to make serious and sometimes challenging points. He is no great admirer of the consumer society and has expressed himself forcefully on the need for the just and humane treatment of the unemployed and on the fundamental right to work. Talks are, naturally, conducted with the greatest courtesy and the visitors leave knowing that they have been listened to with interest and attention and that whatever the Pope can do to help them will be done gladly.

Top left: *the Pope greets Soviet cosmonauts A.S. Aliseyev and Valeri Ryumin who were in Rome for the Congress of the International Astronautical Federation.*
Top: *Tanzanian President Julius Nyerere values Pope John Paul's strong support for Third World countries.*
Above left: *Mr Norman St John-Stevas talks over plans for his forthcoming biography of the Pope.*
Above: *the Pope admires a present brought by Lord Grade.*

VATICAN GARDENS

Shortly after Pope John Paul moved into the Vatican he began to make it his business to get to know as many as possible of the men and women who work behind the scenes. The Vatican has its own printing works where the official newspaper *Osservatore Romano* is produced in several languages, mints its own coinage, prints its own much-prized postage stamps, has an infirmary, a shop, a pharmacy and even a petrol pump. There are more than seven hundred residents of Vatican City and hundreds more who live in the city of Rome come in daily to work in the offices of the Vatican's departments of state and papal commissions and organisations, and at their crafts as carpenters, picture restorers, tapestry weavers, mosaic specialists, masons, painters and decorators.

The entire Vatican territory, the smallest independent state in the world and only slightly larger than London's St James's Park, covers little more than one hundred acres, one third of it given over to gardens. The gardeners were well placed to observe the new Pope as he walked briskly up and down the hilly paths of his little domain, visiting the numerous buildings that are scattered about the grounds.

In those early days, Pope John Paul often stopped to chat with the garden staff, and took a keen though regretful interest in the work on which most of them were then engaged, the felling of oak trees that had been attacked by disease. Veteran gardeners were no strangers to conversations with popes. Several of them remembered how much Pope John XXIII admired the beds of brilliantly coloured flowers and the superb collection of roses, and how animatedly he would make suggestions and enquire about plans for future seasons. In his day, there were eighty gardeners.

Pope Paul VI was very different. He had no great interest in the gardens and his determination to simplify and make economies led to changes. As gardeners reached retiring age or took jobs elsewhere, they were not replaced and today the staff numbers only twenty seven. Inevitably it has been necessary to reduce the amount of work. The flower beds and rose arbours are no more, and the gardens Pope John Paul sees as his helicopter circles before landing, or when he gazes out from his roof terrace, though they are as beautifully tended as ever, consist principally of easily maintained lawns with dwarf wisterias, perpetual flowering jasmine and unassuming beds of pansies giving the few accents of colour. Today they are green gardens, though full of lovely vistas.

The walls that encircle the Vatican were built a thousand years ago to protect the church of St Peter from Saracen pirates who regularly landed at the ancient port of Ostia and descended on Rome for sack and pillage. The land behind the church was left in its natural wild state because the popes traditionally lived in the now vanished

Facing page, above: *the Vatican gardens viewed from the dome of St Peter's. Pope John Paul's coat of arms is in a raised bed in front of the Governor's Palace where the Pontifical Commission for the Vatican City State has its headquarters.*
Below: *a characteristic corner of the gardens. In the foreground, a statue of St Peter, the oddly shaped Eagle fountain beyond and shady groves of trees that give tranquillity and peace.*

Lateran Palace and it was only after 1377 that they took up residence in the Vatican.

Though the great walls were strengthened and widened during the fifteenth century, and again in the sixteenth when the present basilica of St Peter's was being built, the gardens were never landscaped to an overall plan but have evolved over the centuries with the popes of the day adding buildings or fountains or planting trees or copses according to their tastes and interests.

Despite the lack of planning, the Vatican gardens are remarkably attractive. There are charming groups of chestnuts, oaks and olives and shady avenues where earlier popes used to stroll in the summer; several notable fountains, including one of the very finest in Rome, the Galleon fountain, and one of the most criticised, the Eagle fountain; and graceful statues, some of them set round with palm trees. The rock garden has many rare specimen plants and an Eritrean pepper whose July flowers are a magnificent shower of scarlet.

There is also a pretty little enclosed grove of orange and lemon trees, underplanted with a kitchen garden where salad plants, beans, cabbages and tomatoes flourish. The kitchen garden was established in the last century by Pope Leo XIII. This part of the gardens has been reduced also but still supplies vegetables in season for the Pope's household.

The handsome palaces linked by winding paths, have for many years served as offices for pontifical commissions. The exquisite garden house of Pope Pius IV is nowadays the seat of the papal Academy of Sciences, a forum to which distinguished international experts are invited. In the last few years, several important conferences have been held there, including a major conference on the treatment of cancer.

It was from here that last December Pope John Paul sent delegates to visit heads of state from all over the world to present documents drawn up by the Academy setting out the physical and psychological dangers of any nuclear conflict. Another important body, the commission for Archaeological Studies and Research which was

Above: the Italian garden is a huge, formally patterned green carpet of low, clipped hedges enclosing mown grass, gravel paths and basin fountains.
Facing page, above: *beyond the Vatican radio station this shady walk climbs the hill to the south-west summit of the gardens. The helicopter landing site is just behind the tower.*
Below: *the Galleon fountain is a magnificent, fifteen foot long scale model of a seventeenth-century warship. The three masts carry copper rigging and brass sails. The jets from the cannon and the spray rising from the poop deck imitate the smoke of battle. It was designed by a Flemish artist in about 1620.*

set up by Pope John XXIII, also has its headquarters in the gardens, in a manor house that incorporates a mediaeval tower.

From the top of the highest hill soars the tall mast of the Vatican radio station. Pope John Paul has many times broadcast from here, ever since his first days as a young bishop at the Council. Vatican Radio puts out programmes in more than thirty languages and is on the air for twenty hours out of twenty four. Its signature tune, the refrain of "Christus Vincit", is known all over the world and can be heard in this country introducing its thrice daily broadcasts in English.

Not far away is the helicopter landing strip, in use more than ever these days as Pope John Paul flies back and forth to Castelgandolfo, the country palace fifteen miles south-east of Rome which, unlike other popes, he uses all the year round – as much as anything because the swimming pool that has been built there enables him to take the strenuous exercise that is still a medical necessity. Pope Paul VI gave orders for the landing strip to be built after the embarrassment caused when the helicopter in which President Nixon had arrived sank gently into the soft level ground and proved extremely difficult to extricate.

The gardens are very marshy between the hills and in past centuries the whole area was regarded as most unhealthy. To avoid the difficulties the architect encountered when the new audience hall was being built, the helicopter strip was laid out on one of the highest points available, just inside the walls. The Pope's arrivals and departures are the subject of considerable interest to the families who live in the tall blocks of flats that overlook the garden.

People visiting the gardens are often surprised to see the white marble platform of a railway station and are intrigued by the absence of a ticket office. The Vatican has its own branch line, connected to the national railway network. Passengers, though, are rare as the station is mostly used for receiving goods and sending supplies and documents to papal embassies abroad. Another modern improvement is the fine

Below: a rather battered looking Eagle averts his gaze from the fountain that bears his name, an interesting rather than harmonious group of rustic grottoes and tumbling cascades built about 1612.

tennis court, formerly a bowling green, approached by an elegant staircase. It is used by Vatican residents.

Though in the past Pope John Paul was sometimes to be seen walking with his Polish secretary, Monsignor Dziwisz, along the upper paths of the gardens, his schedule these days is so packed that he seldom has time to visit them on foot. When he is in the gardens he is usually en route to his helicopter to make a journey outside Rome and almost invariably this will be in the afternoons. As the gardens are only open to the public in the mornings, tourists have little chance of an unexpected encounter.

Most visitors take the guided coach tour which saves them the effort of climbing the steeper paths. However, free tickets to the gardens are easily obtained by writing to the Pontifical Commission for the Vatican City State, giving the proposed date and the number of people in your party. You will feel a very distinguished guest indeed when you present yourselves at the entrance and receive the smart and courteous salute of the Swiss Guards.

The tranquillity of the Vatican gardens is in wonderfully peaceful contrast to the bustle of Rome. Although official traffic is allowed, cars and delivery vans are required to be driven at a very slow pace and as there are so few vehicles the typically Italian sound of an insistently blaring horn is never heard. The absence of noise has encouraged wild life. Lizards are everywhere and there are far more birds than are generally seen in Italian cities. As well as doves, sparrows and blackbirds, the keen-eyed visitor may also glimpse one of the three brightly coloured parrots that are known to live in the woods. They are thought to have escaped from nearby houses and can sometimes be seen perched high on the branches of the taller trees.

One of the most recent additions to the gardens is a parterre depicting the Pope's coat of arms. The shield is carried out in a dark evergreen and a golden variety of the same species forms the cross and the letter M – in honour of Mary.

Above: *the Casina of Pope Pius IV is a beautiful two-storey classical villa that has a matching pavilion as a summer house. Built in 1560, the Casina today houses the pontifical Academy of Sciences.*

ALL IN
A DAY'S WORK

Pope John Paul rises early. By five a.m. the shutters of his bedroom on the north-east side of the Vatican Palace are wide open. He starts the day with personal prayer, then recites the morning office that every priest says before carrying out the vigorous exercise programme recommended by his doctor some years ago to prevent the risk of a blood disorder recurring. The athletic Pope enjoys his workout and finishes with an ice-cold shower, winter and summer.

At seven a.m. he says Mass in his small private chapel, in the presence of his two priest-secretaries, Father John Magee from Northern Ireland and the Polish Stanislas Dziwisz, and the three nuns who came from Cracow to look after the domestic arrangements of his household. There may also be friends and guests who have stayed overnight. Pope John Paul invites any priests to celebrate Mass with him at the altar – in the language, often English, in which the others are most at ease.

Breakfast is informal. The Pope has a hearty appetite for ham sliced very thin, fried eggs, rolls, fruit and coffee. By eight-thirty the secretaries join him in his study with drafts and documents and a press summary from the world's newspapers. Audiences begin at ten-thirty, half an hour earlier than originally planned, in the rather vain hope that they won't overrun the morning time-table. Foreign and state visitors are, of course, always received punctually but seldom leave on time, as the Pope and his callers always find so much to discuss.

The five or six cardinals, archbishops and bishops from all over the world who arrive by appointment have learned to be philosophical when they are kept waiting. He greets each one warmly and, though he may start behind his desk with his visitor to one side, very soon slides his chair along the carpet until they are sitting companionably close. He will stretch out to pat his guest's arm while he listens, nodding his head at each point made and asking question after question. It is generally nearly two o'clock before he will look at his watch, spring out of his chair, ask his visitor if he can stay to lunch, scoop the papers they have been discussing into a pile and, throwing his arm round the other's shoulder, usher him briskly along the corridor.

Lunch is served in the small dining room where there is a table that seats six and a television set in one corner. When only his secretaries are with him, they watch one of the cassette recordings of his overseas visits and make notes that will smooth out arrangements for the next journey. On most days there will be guests, friends from Poland and colleagues who are in Rome briefly and have been invited by telephone just the previous day.

Afterwards Pope John Paul takes a short break in the open air. He likes to go up on the roof terrace overlooking the Vatican gardens and spend a little time alone in reflection and prayer. By four o'clock he is back in his study receiving his special visitors – people who are very close to him, others who have asked for his help and intervention, emissaries whose business is highly confidential.

His secretaries join him an hour later with the day's correspondence – the Pope personally sees everything of importance. After that he prepares addresses and sermons for the next few days or works on the important encyclical letters that express his thought and teaching. In the early evening he sees his Secretary of State, Cardinal Casaroli, to talk over international issues that affect the Catholic Church.

Pope John Paul goes again to his private chapel at about eight o'clock and recites the Rosary aloud with all the members of his household, joined by any friends who have come in good time for supper. He always has company in the evenings. As well as priests, he sometimes invites family groups and his apartments ring with the laughter of young voices and the melodies of Polish folk songs.

A little after ten o'clock he says farewell to his guests with a blessing, then goes to his room to read for another hour, usually with classical music playing in the background, before he goes to bed. It has been a long day and he sleeps well.

Signing the second encyclical letter. Written in Latin and addressed to the whole Church, papal encyclicals set out Roman Catholic teaching in great detail. Pope John Paul's first two encyclicals, Redemptor Hominis (Redeemer of Man) issued in March 1979 and Dives in Misericordia (Riches in Mercy) issued in December 1980, dealt with matters of doctrine. The third, Laborem Exercens (On Human Work) issued September 1981, was a major statement on the fundamental right to work and all its implications for the individual and society.

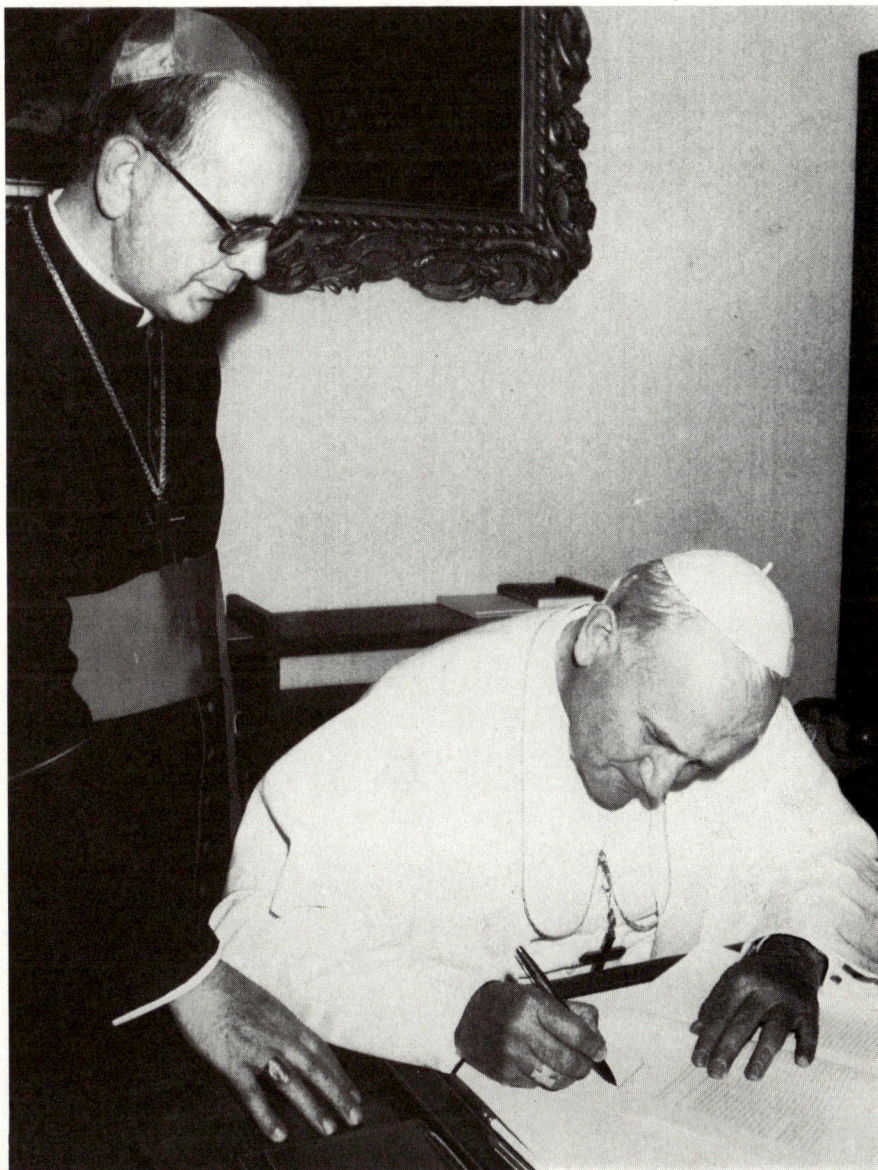

FACE TO FACE

When a pope is elected he becomes Bishop of Rome and inherits many other titles. Some are mainly of historic interest but one has very great significance – Servus Servorum Dei, servant of the servants of God. Pope John Paul's approach to his high task is to give equal importance to both callings and to make himself available as bishop and servant to everyone who lives in or comes to Rome. And being the man he is, he interprets availability as going out to make personal contact. There has never been a pope who has been so eager to meet people, and certainly no pope before John Paul has proved such a magnetic attraction. All people, it seems, want to share his company and meet him face to face.

Every Wednesday the Pope holds an audience for all who care to come and meet him. Anyone can obtain a ticket entitling him to a seat by going along a couple of days beforehand to one of the Vatican departments. Most people, though, come in organised groups. Audiences used to be held inside St Peter's and later in the new audience hall built in 1971 behind the left wing of the colonnade and with much better facilities for seeing and hearing clearly. The hall, and sometimes the basilica, is still used during the winter, but Pope John Paul's general audiences are so well attended that as far as possible they are held outdoors in the huge Piazza where as many as a hundred thousand can find room.

Sturdy wooden barriers are placed in position to divide the Piazza into sections and from two hours beforehand pilgrimage parties, parish groups and visitors from all over pour in to take their seats. Invalids and people in wheelchairs are escorted to a place of honour close to the big central dais where the Pope will sit, and are greeted by very smart salutes from the Swiss Guards in their picturesque dress uniforms of red, yellow and blue striped tunics and breeches, stiff ruffs and high-tilted black berets. Dozens of officials are on hand to cope with the huge throng: papal ushers in black tail coats, grey-uniformed members of the society of volunteer stewards, officers of the little Vatican police force and the endlessly patient young soldiers of the Swiss Guard, steer the groups into their appointed places and reassure their anxious leaders that they will all be able to see well.

There is a tremendously festive atmosphere and a great hubbub of excited comment as people find their seats, abandon them, mill around in the enclosures and photograph the lively cosmopolitan scene. Many groups carry placards lettered with the name of their country or parish or organisation and there is much jolly brandishing of national flags – the Polish flag is always much in evidence. Scores of people are carrying presents for the Pope. Framed pictures and statues of the Virgin are a popular choice, for his fondness for visiting shrines where she is particularly

Last October British bobbies from St Albans attended a Wednesday audience to deliver thousands of letters written to the Pope by schoolchildren, as part of a sponsored drive to raise funds for a centre for the mentally handicapped. The Pope congratulated them on their charitable work. The father of the only English Pope is buried in the Abbey at St Albans. Nicholas Breakspear was Pope Adrian IV from 1154-1159.

54

honoured is well known. But there are many humble hand-made gifts — long loaves of Polish bread patterned with poppy seeds and bunches of flowers by the dozen.

Sacred music is broadcast for the last half-hour of waiting and then, ten minutes before the Pope is due, an honour party of six Swiss Guards in red-plumed helmets and holding silver-bladed lances marches out from an archway to take up position either side of the central dais. Vatican carpenters appear and prudently bolt the barrier sections firmly together to make them immovable, to the good-humoured regret and friendly protests of people who have strategically stationed themselves against the barriers perhaps with the thought of pushing them aside just as soon as the Pope arrives and having a personal word without delay.

At eleven o'clock the white jeep comes in sight and enters the Piazza through the Arch of the Bells and the Pope, standing and smiling with his hand raised in blessing, drives at walking pace through the barricaded aisles to roars of welcome and applause. After slowly circling the entire Piazza and greeting the thousands who have arrived without tickets and are standing in the space between the fountains, he drives back to the centre where he leaves the jeep and walks up the main aisle, stopping to talk several times on the way, and mounts the steps to the dais to take his seat in a high-backed armchair.

He then preaches for ten or fifteen minutes, speaking in Italian but giving summaries of his theme in English, German, French, Spanish and Polish as he goes along. Since the attempt on his life, he has shared his reflections on the spiritual value of this experience of suffering and his gratitude for the prayers of the world. Often he takes as his subject the events of the day, interpreting joys and tragedies and relating them to God's values.

After the address, Vatican officials come to the microphone to offer greetings on behalf of various groups present: missionary brothers, a pilgrimage from Brazil, a conference of American physicians, parish groups from many parts of Italy, a choir from France, student priests from the beleaguered Church in Hungary, undergraduates from Warsaw University, a diocesan pilgrimage from England, a party of fund-raisers for charity. As each group is named, the members jump to their feet and wave and clap their greetings, and the Pope smiles back his encouragement and acknowledgement, punching the air with emphatic gestures of his clasped hands and leading the rest of the crowd in applause.

Sometimes a group will burst into a few verses of a hymn and Pope John Paul, who

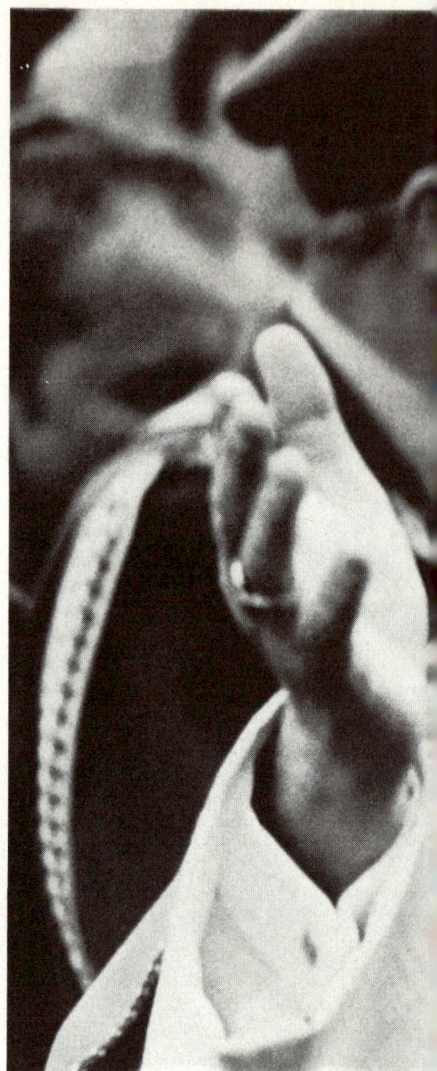

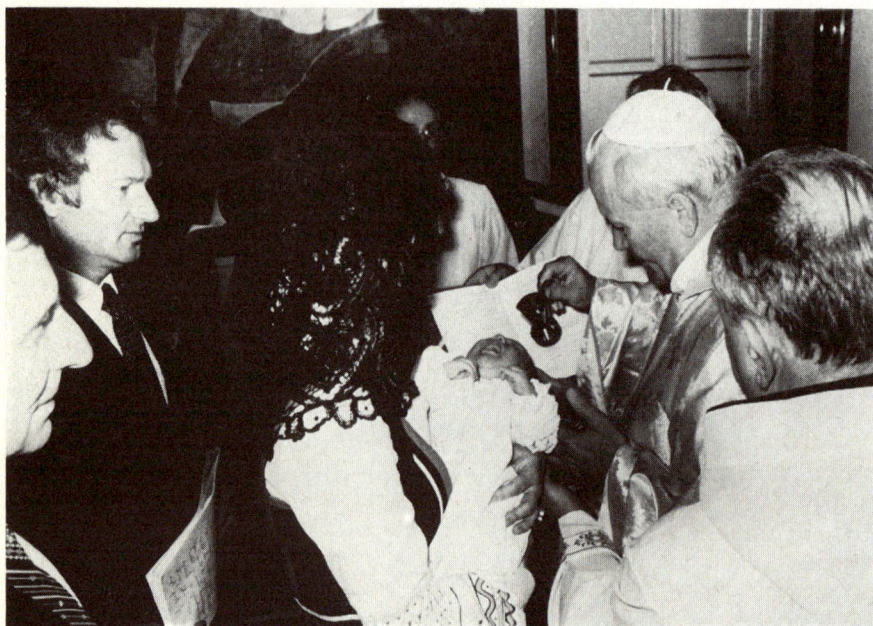

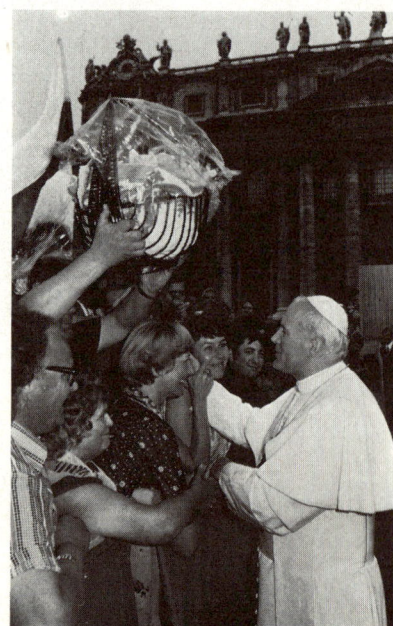

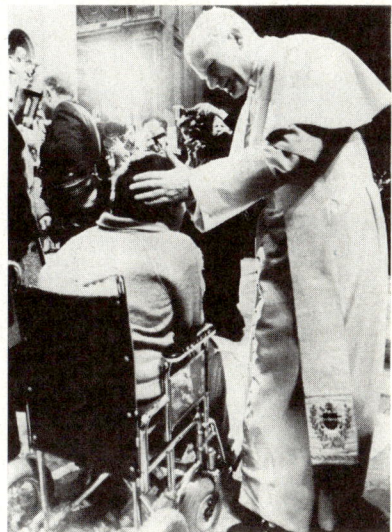

seems to have an amazing repertoire of songs, hums the tune along with them. The formal part of the audience ends with a solemn blessing. If there are cardinals and bishops present, the Pope will urge them to join him on the dais and pronounce the blessing together with him. It is a vivid demonstration of the universality of the Church, for there are almost sure to be Africans and Asians as well as Europeans among them.

From the point of view of many in the Piazza, the best is yet to come – the chance of a personal chat and an individual blessing. The Pope comes down to move among the people in a completely easy and informal way. He has a special word and consoling gesture for all the sick, and then walks about for the best part of an hour, greeting everyone as a friend, grasping hundreds of outstretched hands, affectionately stroking the hair of the children who are held out to him and seem so at home with him that they often twine their arms round his neck and need a good deal of disentangling – during which the little white skullcap is a frequent casualty.

He accepts with genuine pleasure all the gifts that are offered, inspects and admires them thoroughly and gratefully thanks the givers before their offerings are borne away to be placed on a long table – and later given to charity. When at length he leaves to mount his jeep, everyone there has the same impression: that Pope John Paul is a man in love with people and radiant with the joy of serving them.

There are nearly three hundred parishes in Rome and their Bishop the Pope is well

Facing page, far left: Stephen and Janina Buller booked a papal baptism months before Alexis was born.
Left: Polish pilgrims offer a splendid basket of fruit and wine.
Above left: Pope John Paul may greet as many as eighty thousand people at a public audience in the Piazza.
Top: all the magnificence of St Peter's and this little girl feels quite at home hand in hand with the Holy Father.
Above: handicapped and invalids have a place of honour and are singled out with fatherly affection.

embarked on a systematic plan of spending time with their people. Shortly after becoming Pope, he held a three-hour meeting at his new cathedral church in Rome, St John Lateran. A large number of the eleven hundred priests engaged in pastoral work among the three million inhabitants of Rome were invited. The new Pope freely confessed that the diocese was almost unknown to him. All his previous time in Rome had been spent as a student or as a Polish bishop attending conferences. He asked for as much information as they could give him and encouraged a very free and frank discussion.

Priests who had expected to be addressed rather than listened to were surprised to find themselves doing most of the talking. They were surprised, too, by Pope John Paul's penetrating questions about housing conditions, unemployment, practical facilities to help working families, and what was being done to help young people to find meaning in their lives. Most popes have come from long years of work in the governmental organisation or the diplomatic service of the Church and seemed worlds away from the realities of parish work.

Since that meeting the Pope has made a practice of spending every free Sunday at one of his Rome parishes. A few days beforehand, the parish priest and his curates are invited to supper at the Vatican to talk over plans for the coming visit. The Pope asks particularly about arrangements for him to meet people who are in personal difficulties and, should there be a prison, a remand home or a hostel for rehabilitating drug offenders within the parish, he makes certain of going there. The inmates are touchingly glad to see him and are greatly cheered by his spontaneous and affectionate pleasure in the gifts they have prepared.

Young drug addicts who had worked hard in the carpentry shop to make him a marquetry picture of the famous ikon of Our Lady of Czestochowa had their fragile self-esteem hugely boosted by the way Pope John Paul hugged the picture to himself

Above left: *raising the Host at an open air Mass. As Bishop of Rome, the Pope takes every opportunity to visit one of his three hundred parishes.*
Above: *the wedding of a Roman dustman's daughter and her electrician bridegroom. A few months after taking office, Pope John Paul married Virginia and Mario Maltese in the Vatican's Pauline chapel.*
Above right: *children from the Roman parish of Santa Croce in Gerusalemme greet the Holy Father with balloons, smiles and outstretched hands.*
Right: *a bewildered baby too young to know he is in the arms of the Pope himself, an expert cuddler of "bambini".*

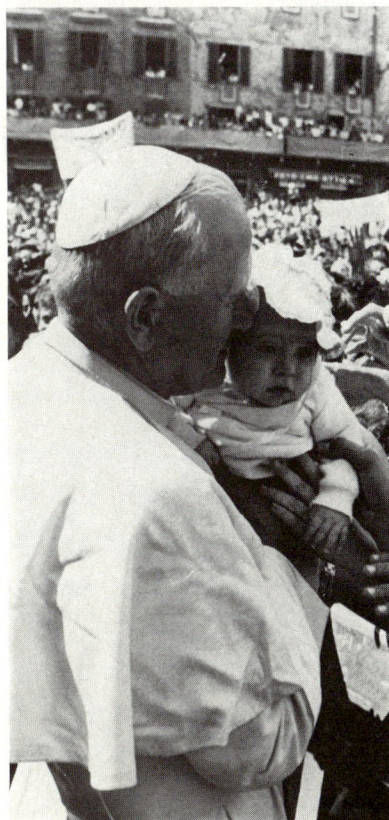

and only reluctantly surrendered it in order to shake hands with them all. Hospitals and maternity homes are always on his list, and new babies who time their arrivals well are likely to find themselves being baptised by His Holiness.

Every parish visit the Pope makes is a day of great celebration. When he arrives he is welcomed with a display of banners made by the schoolchildren, and carefully lettered as he would like with "greetings to our Bishop". At the church he concelebrates evening Mass with the local clergy and will read the gospel of the day and preach, if invited. Again and again his theme is the building of a community of love and service. His visits are a powerful impetus in bringing people together as they organise decorations, rehearse dances and songs for the concert that invariably takes place, and prepare festive suppers for all-comers.

One Roman parish was lucky enough to receive the Pope on May 18th, his birthday and the day on which the foundation stone of their church was laid in 1920, the year of his birth. Centrepiece of that festive supper was a vast birthday cake in the shape of a flight of steps leading up to a tower crowned by a model of the parish church. It had been made by the local pastry cook with half the parish helping. Before he blew out the candle on the lowest step, the Pope delighted all the youngsters when he said that he could only accept the cake if all of them would promise to think of other children round the world who had to go hungry, give him a hand to help them – and also give him a bit of assistance in helping to eat the cake.

Pope John Paul's progress round his three hundred parishes will take some time to complete at his present rate of twenty visits a year. After the attempt on his life last May, all engagements were indefinitely postponed. But within a few days of his return to full-time work at the Vatican in early October, he had already set in motion plans to resume his visits, and within a fortnight was back on his rounds. His doctors shook their heads but his people were gratified.

59

EVERY SUNDAY IN ROME

Visitors to Rome have a favourite Sunday morning tradition: to go to St Peter's Square at midday and say the Angelus prayers with the Pope and receive his blessing. The Angelus prayers take their name from the account given in the first chapter of St Luke's Gospel: "the angel of the Lord declared unto Mary". They go back to the fourteenth century and were a lay adaptation of the thrice-daily prayers said in monasteries. Pope John Paul's Angelus is well loved because as well as leading the familiar prayers he nearly always gives a short address. Sometimes he preaches about the prayers, or comments on the life of the saint who is commemorated that day. Or he may take the assembled people into his confidence with a report on a recent overseas visit, or announce plans for another journey that has not even been rumoured.

The audience at his Angelus were the first to know that he intended to go to Turkey, though only the best informed understood the significance of a pope going to a country with a secular constitution, where most of the people are Moslems, in order to further fraternal ties with the Orthodox Patriarch of Constantinople. Everyone responded to the appeal he made at another Angelus ceremony for prayers for the safety of the young English girl Annabel Schild, held captive by bandits in Sardinia. On that occasion his influence was decisive and Annabel was released.

Long before twelve o'clock thousands are already waiting in the Piazza for the homely half-hour ceremony. Tourist buses draw up and people pour out and wander around, not quite sure exactly what it is they have been advised to come and see and asking each other about the best place to stand. Those who have spent the morning visiting the great basilica stream out from the doors and down the wide steps to gather near the entrance to the Piazza.

There is always a large turn-out of invalids and disabled people and it is interesting to see how self-assured so many of them are in asking their helpers, or sometimes complete strangers, to move them to where the Pope will notice them. They are proudly aware of being people for whom he has marked regard. Family parties stroll around. Children play by the fountains and swarm up the steps of the obelisk for the best view of their friend.

The Pope's apartments are on the second floor of the Palace that rises behind the right wing of the colonnade. Fifteen minutes before Angelus time the casement windows of his private study are opened and a long red velvet banner with his crest in gold and a gold-braided double border is hung from the window-sill. As the banner ripples in the breeze, attendants can be seen placing a microphone and a Perspex reading desk in position. The expectant people mass more densely, binoculars are

Above: gathering by the lovely Carlo Maderno fountain in St Peter's Square to take part in the midday Angelus. This, the earlier of the two fountains, is nearer the Vatican Palace.
Facing page: Pope John Paul begins to sing the Blessing "In the name of the Father . . ." at Sunday Angelus.

readied and thousands of cameras focused. When the clock of St Peter's begins to chime the hour, pigeons fly up in alarm and wheel round the Piazza, some settling on the Vatican Palace just by the Pope's window for the best vantage-point of all.

On the stroke of twelve, Pope John Paul comes to the window, and smiling, throws his arms wide in greeting. The thousands in the Piazza, sometimes as many as eighty thousand, applaud tumultuously, wave hands and handkerchiefs, banners and balloons and shout their enthusiasm. The Pope does not encourage prolonged personal applause and stills the assembly immediately, makes the sign of the cross and begins at once, "Praised be Jesus Christ".

Then he preaches, perhaps on the gospel and psalms read at morning mass, or on the words of the prayers that they are about to say together that acknowledge the power of God to change lives. His words are simple, direct and profound and he is listened to with attention by everyone with a smattering of Italian, and with respect by those non-Italians who, unable to understand what is being said, are nonetheless held by the power of his resonant voice. When he begins the Angelus prayers, the responses come loudly and confidently from all over the Piazza and most feelingly from the groups of his own countrymen who are always there in great numbers.

Pope John Paul takes great pains to be well briefed about the various national and religious groups who have let him know that they will be with him on Sunday. He addresses special greetings to them all, and always to the young people, the sick and the handicapped. As soon as he says "Bambini . . ." excited cries and shrieks resound because all the children know very well what favourites they are.

To the people from abroad the Pope then speaks in their own languages. In his

Those who can follow Italian listen attentively to the Pope's address which makes Sunday Angelus so popular. But he adds messages and blessings in many other languages.

On the stroke of twelve Pope John Paul comes to the window of his private study. A red velvet banner adorned with his coat of arms in gold braid hangs from the window sill.

slow, careful English he may say, "This Sunday Angelus gives all of us the opportunity to gather in the name of the Lord Jesus and to honour his Blessed Mother in our prayers. I pray that the English speaking visitors will be strengthened in their faith and find renewed joy in the community of Christ's Church. To all of you, grace and peace." People enthusiastically applaud his greetings and strangers smile at each other, exhilarated by the pleasure they see on every face.

When the Pope begins to sing the blessing, in Latin, the crowd falter a little over the responses, but as he makes the sign of the cross all join in a responding Amen. Cheers break out, the Pope waves again and adds a homely comment about the good or bad weather as he keenly gazes down.

Then with a last wave he turns and goes inside. Seconds later the window banner is hauled in, the casements closed, the light curtains drawn against the sun. The people linger, just in case he should return, then slowly begin to drift away. "I saw him," a little boy shouts excitedly, "and I think he saw me." It has been a very happy half-hour for everyone.

ENCIRCLING THE WORLD

Within fifteen weeks of his election Pope John Paul had set off on the first of his missionary journeys. Before his departure he spoke of his desire to be a messenger of the gospel "for the millions of brothers and sisters who believe in Christ. The Pope wants to know them, embrace them and tell them all – children, young people, men, women, workers, peasants, professionals – that God loves them, that the Church loves them, that the Pope loves them, and he wants to receive from them the encouragement and example of their goodness, their faith." From the outset he made it clear he sought dialogue.

On Thursday January 25th 1979 he stepped down from the Alitalia aircraft painted with his new coat of arms that had brought him to Santo Domingo. Kneeling at the foot of the aircraft steps he prostrated himself full length to kiss the soil of Latin America. This gesture of humble respect which has since become so familiar was no flamboyant impulse. "Pope Paul VI was accustomed after alighting from the plane to begin his visit by kissing the ground." he recalled. "I think this

Below: wherever his missionary journeys take him the Pope's first action is to kneel and kiss God's earth, as a sign of humble respect and of the universality of the Church serving all men.
Facing page: Pope John Paul reads and prays as he flies from Rome to Santo Domingo, capital of the Dominican Republic, en route for Mexico. He undertook this first overseas journey in January 1979, shortly after his election.

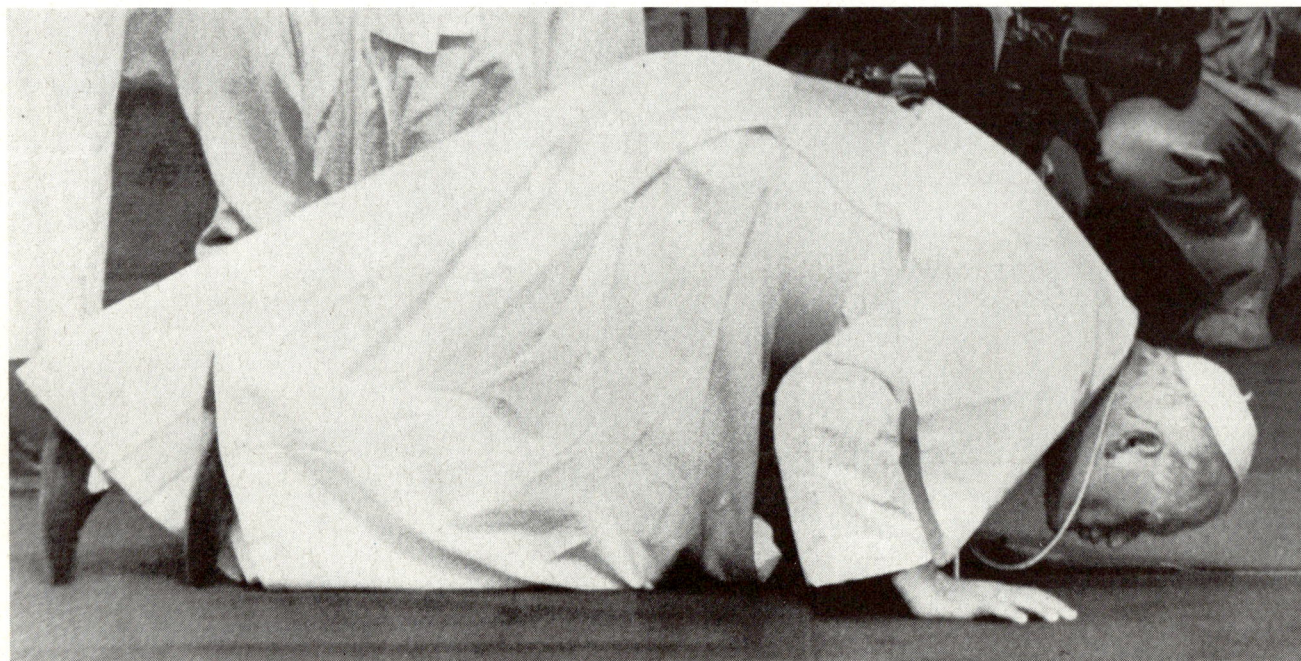

Right: *arriving at Warsaw airport. In June 1979 he returned to his homeland as Pope, in an Alitalia plane bearing his coat of arms. Behind him are Cardinal Wyszynski who had gone on board to welcome him, his Secretary of State Cardinal Casaroli and his secretary Monsignor Dziwisz.*
Facing page: *happy to be home, Pope John Paul greets a welcoming crowd. Everywhere banners in Polish scarlet and white and papal yellow and white decorated the churches.*

gesture expresses precisely what the psalm proclaims: Let us bow, prostrate ourselves and kneel in front of the Lord our Maker.''

The Pope was en route for Mexico to address an important conference of Latin American bishops and strengthen them in determining how to lead their people in the face of grave social evils and repressive regimes. Opening the conference in the city of Puebla, his address carried not only the authority of his office but the experience of his own thirty years' struggle to build a Christian community in social conditions of total hostility. He called urgently and passionately for full human rights for the poor and the oppressed but held firmly to the values of the gospels as the only true way to justice and peace.

Long before he arrived in Puebla he had already conquered Mexican hearts. People strewed flowers in his way, everywhere flags and banners flourished a welcome. The exuberance and enthusiasm of the crowds as they sang to ''Juan Pablo'' astonished the local television commentators who had certainly not expected to see the notoriously late-rising Mexicans out in their thousands at dawn. To the Mexicans John Paul was

Seemingly the whole of Poland came to see their Pope. At the Shrine of Our Lady in the monastery of Jasna Gora at Czestochowa he presided at a conference of Polish bishops. The vast crowd that had attended his open-air Mass the day before stayed on — and were rewarded when he came out to say the Angelus prayers with them.

a brother, a worker-Pope. His evident respect for everyone, his powerful championship of innate human dignity and his open admiration for the richness and variety of their customs and traditions as they sang and danced in spectacular costumes entranced the Mexicans.

In the six days he spent in Mexico Pope John Paul set a pattern for the journeys that were to follow – deep communication with working people, inspiring addresses, words of encouragement to priests and religious brothers and sisters to put themselves more fully at the service of mankind, Masses jointly celebrated with bishops and clergy, visits to the sick and suffering, lively and exhilarating meetings with young people. Speaking to a hundred thousand university students he made some mistakes in his Spanish when, after his formal address, he engaged in a long impromptu dialogue and exclaimed, to their delighted laughter, "As you can see, the Pope too must study a bit harder".

Since then he has been an indefatigable traveller and in nine major journeys has visited many countries throughout four continents. The most remarkable of all was

Right: Auschwitz death camp was in his former diocese of Cracow. Sinister words over the gate say: Work is Freedom. The Pope carries flowers given him by two survivors who walk ahead wearing prison uniforms. More than a million people attended his Mass here.

his return to Poland. When Cardinal Wyszynski invited him to be present at the ninth centenary celebrations of the martyrdom of St Stanislas, Bishop of Cracow, that were to take place in May 1979, he at once accepted. The authorities were obstructive and insisted on a few days' postponement so that, as it happened, the Pope returned to his own people on the eve of Pentecost, the birthday of the Church. The intensity of emotion that his presence aroused was quite astonishing to witness and, through reports and pictures filed by the huge international press contingent that followed him everywhere, riveted world attention.

Polish official circles played down the visit and made it as difficult as possible for people to know details of the itinerary. But the nine days Pope John Paul spent in his homeland saw an outpouring of love and a depth of feeling which proved that the spirit of the nation was indeed Polonia Semper Fidelis, ever-faithful Poland – in spite of its tragic history, a land of unshaken belief in the Catholic religion that united old and young, country people and workers from mines and factories, ordinary families, students and intellectuals. From his first tumultuous welcome in Warsaw, where he preached to a huge congregation on the marvellous design of Providence that at the millenium of Christianity in Poland a son of Poland should have been called to the chair of St Peter, to his final Mass for the martyred St Stanislas, whose successor he had himself been as Archbishop of Cracow, Pope John Paul was hailed by millions the length and breadth of the land.

By order of the regime cities were closed off, roads blocked, transport withdrawn, workers threatened with sanctions, school children tempted with promises of outings to try to limit attendances. But everywhere there was the same inspiring determination to be with him and to pray with him. More than a million walked in blazing heat to the Sanctuary of Our Lady in the monastery of Jasna Gora in

Above: in prayer at the Wall of Death where countless thousands were lined up and shot. Hundreds of Polish priests were among the four million exterminated. Pope John Paul knelt in silent prayer for several minutes. Pointing to a plaque in honour of Jewish victims, he declared: "No one can pass by this inscription with indifference."

71

Right: he addressed the nuns of his old diocese in the beautiful Gothic church of St Mary in Cracow. Behind him are mediaeval life-size figures carved by the Polish master Wit Stwosz.
Facing page: with a smile not far away from tears Pope John Paul listens to well loved student songs as the undergraduates of Cracow and the priests serenade their Karolek once again.

Czestochowa to attend an open-air Mass, amongst them a tremendous procession of miners from Silesia where the Pope had been forbidden to go. As many again were with him at Auschwitz to see him celebrate Mass with a dozen priest-survivors and hear his call to remember the horrors of the past in order to pray the more fervently that never again should such things happen.

His welcome home to his own Cracow where the whole population stood for hours in pouring rain to be ready for his typically late arrival, and where his old students serenaded him till he came out on the balcony to laugh and sing with them, was like a great family party. His open-air Mass at Nowy Targ, high in the mountains near Czechoslovakia where he had so often gone to climb and ski, was a triumph against all odds. Official permission for any preparation was refused until apparently too late. Undeterred, local people rushed planks sawn in secret up the mountains overnight and built a spectacular open church in the shape of the high-pitched wooden roof of a mountaineer's hut, above a simple altar. Though thousands were turned back at the Czechoslovak border, the crowd was vast.

After the service they sang in farewell a famous Polish folk-song about the highlander in exile and how he must grieve for the loss of the streams and mountains he knew in the land of his birth. When he returned to Rome Pope John Paul spoke of

In the high hills of Mexico. Pope John Paul's first journey took him from Mexico City, largest city in the world, to Indian villages, great shrines of Our Lady and the huge industrial centre of Monterey where several hundred thousand workers hailed him as the worker-Pope.

In Chicago Pope John Paul had nine major engagements. He presided over a meeting of three hundred and fifty bishops and more than a million came to the Mass he celebrated at Grant Park.

private chat, address Congress, preside at an ecumenical meeting of several thousand delegates from Christian churches all over the land, speak to the Organisation of American States and have a tremendously successful get-together with thousands of university students. When they began to chant "John Paul II, we like you" the Pope sang back "John Paul II likes you too!" The students had held an all-night prayer vigil to ask God's blessing on their encounter, an endeavour that the Pope described as a wonderful expression of communion with him and a most beautiful gift. Later, speaking to presidents of Catholic colleges and universities, he made a fine plea for academic honesty and intellectual freedom.

Pope John Paul's next international journey, to Turkey, was in total contrast. The Turkish authorities, though correct and courteous, were anything but warm and the Turkish people, except for one sinister young convicted terrorist who issued a death threat, hardly aware that he was there. The Pope described his trip as a fraternal visit to greet the Greek Orthodox Archbishop of Constantinople. Their meeting, rich in the symbolism of reconciliation, may prove to have been a great turning point on the road to Christian reunion.

So, too, may the journey he made a full year later to Germany, the land of Luther. Regarded as potentially divisive, and forecast as likely to be at the very least

politically difficult – the Pope is a Pole and the Nazi death camp at Auschwitz desecrated the land of his own diocese of Cracow – it turned out very differently. His meetings with the representatives of the Protestant churches and communities were most cordial and even the appalling weather could not keep away many thousands of German Catholics.

Earlier, in the spring of 1980, the Pope had spent five days in Zaire, where roughly half the twenty-two million population is Catholic. He visited the Congo Republic, Kenya, Upper Volta, Ghana and the Ivory Coast. Through the steamy heat of the forests, tropical storms in Ghana, desert drought in Upper Volta – where he made a stirring call for more help to be given to famine victims – and in the high altitude of Kenya where at last the tropical heat was less enervating, he showed an unflagging enthusiasm for the vitality of the African church and his customary appreciation of the intensely African character of their celebration of the liturgy. As priests swayed round the altar, tom-toms sounded and offertory processions were transformed into joyous presentations of the fruits of the earth – balanced in baskets on the heads of Africans who danced up the steps to the altar.

In France his dialogue with young people brought his famous declaration of his love for the priestly service: "I've been Pope for two years and a bishop for twenty but

Far left: *a posy of roses, carnations and chrysanthemums in the papal colours of yellow and white was given to Pope John Paul at the Dominican Convent in Cabra, Ireland, where the sisters care for four hundred handicapped children.*
Left above: *blessing a crippled child in the arms of her mother. The Pope said Mass for the sick and suffering at the Shrine of Our Lady in Knock.*
Below: *deep in prayer at the ceremonies in Phoenix Park, Dublin. The intensity of Pope John Paul's concentration during the liturgy of the Mass is striking.*
Right: *from the start of his ten day journey in Africa, where he visited six countries and gave more than seventy addresses, Pope John Paul was besieged by the crowds and often had difficulty in making his way through.*

for me the most important thing is that I'm a priest''. Later in the summer of 1980 he journeyed to Brazil, where his twelve day visit was a marathon of endurance. He spoke as strongly as he had done in Mexico about the dangers of seeing the Church as an instrument of politics – and just as strongly in support of the dignity of every man. He travelled up the Amazon to reach the distressed South American Indians and endorsed the policies of the radical Archbishop Helder Camara, the champion of the poor vilified by the rich and powerful.

He went to a shanty-town parish from which the authorities had wanted to keep him away, and was so overcome by the poverty and wretchedness of the people that he took off his gold ring of office and gave it to the parish priest as a personal pledge of his desire to help materially as well as spiritually. He went to the leper colony of Belem and kissed and embraced the poor patients who had been too fearful of causing offence with their sad disfigurements to venture out.

In the spring of last year Pope John Paul flew to Asia's only Christian country, the Philippines. In the six days he spent there he spoke sternly, in the presence of the President, of the inequalities of Philippine society – and drew a remarkable statement of contrition from President Marcos, who was moved to say "Forgive us, Holy Father" and promise amendment. Eight hundred and fifty thousand Filipinos cheered the Pope as their champion and defender.

He went on to Japan, where the Christian community is tiny. He offended some by calling on the Emperor Hirohito but set criticism aside in favour of respect and

Left: *seated in the welcome shade of a bamboo canopy erected behind the altar where he was to concelebrate Mass. The Zaire priests danced at the altar.*
Below: *Pope John Paul listens intently to a reading from the New Testament. In many of his African sermons he expressed his admiration for cultural traditions.*
Overleaf, left: *on the steps of Notre Dame in Paris the Pope concelebrated Mass with more than a hundred French priests.*
Right: *in the Philippines he admonished the President for breaches of human rights – and found time to embrace one of the youngest of the three-quarter million who came to see and hear him.*

charity. The Catholic community greeted him with great enthusiasm and he was so delighted by the little Japanese children who had learned a faltering version of the popular Polish song of congratulations "Stolat" (May you live for a hundred years) that he seized the microphone to sing it back to them.

But the great event of his Japanese visit was his speech at Hiroshima where survivors of the 1945 atomic bomb still suffer the after-effects. The Pope spoke in Japanese which he had learned for the occasion: "Let us promise our fellow human beings that we will work untiringly for disarmament and the banishing of all nuclear weapons. Let us replace violence and hate with confidence and caring. Let humanity never become the victim of a struggle between competing systems. Let there never be another war."

Pope John Paul has been criticised for travelling too much, as he freely acknowledged when answering blunt questions from a reporter at Vatican Radio. "Speaking from the human point of view," he replied, "they are right. But it is Providence that guides me, and sometimes it suggests that we do certain things to excess." Few in any country visited by this dedicated and loving man would say that he has not spent his time magnificently well. Millions will be glad to see him here.

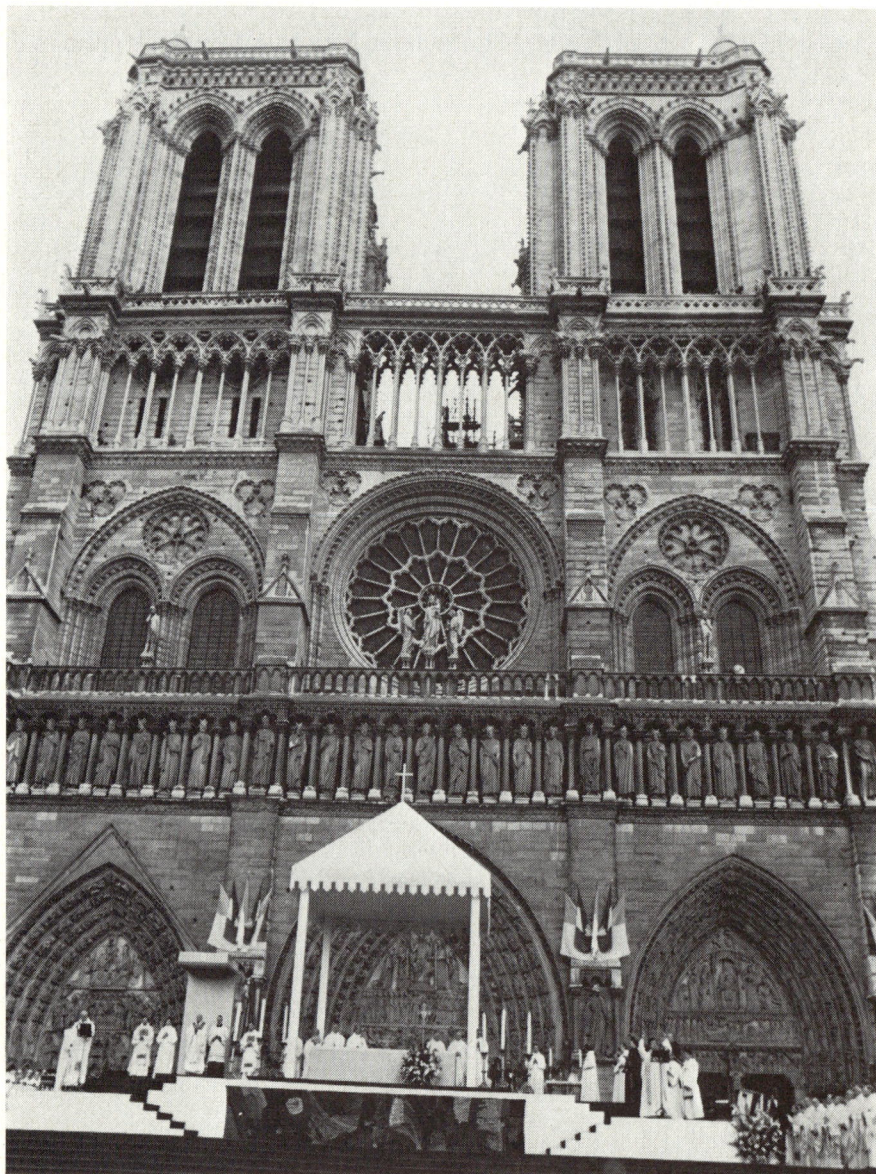

THE
CHILDREN'S POPE

During the surprise walkabout he took after the solemn and dignified ceremonies of his Inauguration Mass, Pope John Paul was mildly mobbed by little boys from Polish families who had rushed up to present him with flowers, quite undeterred by the forbidding glances of disapproving officials. The boys were closely followed by others who ran up too as soon as they saw that all-comers were welcome. It was a very homely scene, with affectionate pats on the head, cheerful hugs and beaming smiles all round. The new pope was already becoming known for his remarkable rapport with children.

To people of a reflective turn of mind this Pied Piper encounter said something very important. While others listed the Pope's intellectual achievements, commenting on the quality and variety of his literary works, analysing the books and essays he had written on doctrine and ethics; and old friends recounted their reminiscences of him as workman, actor, sportsman, pastor, lecturer and linguist; the children saw him simply as a friend, and recognised him unerringly despite the grandeur of the occasion and the magnificence of his robes. And so it has gone on, in every country in the world.

Some of the reasons for Pope John Paul's unusually close relationship with children are not too hard to unravel. His own early years were intensely happy and he learned very young how to give and receive affection. He was in fact so warmly loved by his parents that neighbours who knew the Wojtyla family well used to speculate how this very cherished child would turn out, and suspected that with so much attention focused on him he might easily become extremely self-centred. Any of those neighbours alive today would have to smile at how mistaken their fears were.

Always an exceptionally friendly man, he was one of the family in scores of homes in every parish where he lived and served, and was such a well known figure that none of the children ever thought of needing to be on their best behaviour when he called in unannounced, or came to supper. The children of Cracow were just as free as any one else to go and see him any morning when he held open house in the Archbishop's Palace, and many did so, just for a chat. Which, when you consider it, is a fairly remarkable circumstance. It is thought provoking enough that such an eminent and astonishingly busy man should find time to hear confidences and advise on childish worries; still more surprising, though, that children sought him out.

One of the earliest public audiences he gave, in the midst of all the cares of his new office, was to ten thousand boys and girls from all over Italy. In welcoming them he spoke of how happy he always felt among the young, and gave the reason, fundamental to all he is and does, the example of Christ: "The Pope wishes well to

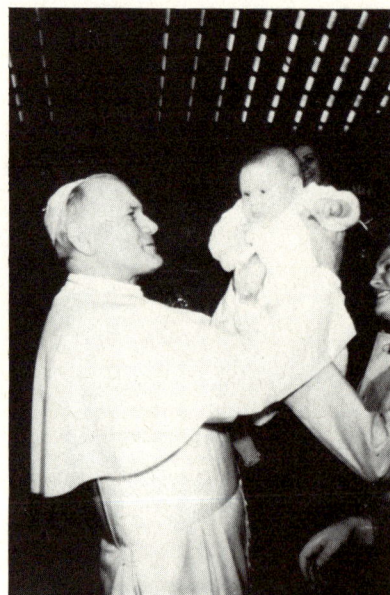

Above: *the children's Pope admires a new young friend, a happy scene that is repeated wherever he goes.*
Right: *in animated man-to-man conversation a little boy with shining eyes chats confidently, hand in hand with the Holy Father.*

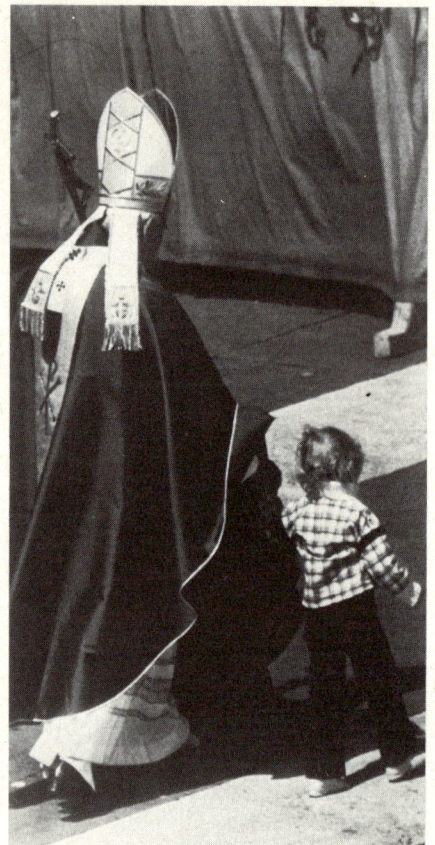

everyone, to each man and to all men, but he has a preference for the youngest because they had a special place in the heart of Christ, who wished to remain with the children and talk to the young. He addressed his call to the young particularly and John, the youngest apostle, was his favourite."

To Pope John Paul every child is a person to love and befriend, and children understand this. Many who run up to him on public occasions are certainly encouraged to do so by their parents, but as soon as they are with him it is as if they had known him all their lives, holding his hand and chatting away without a hint of shyness. Often they will bring presents of flowers, but from time to time he gets offers of cuddly toys and balloons, and even packets of sweets. He is adept at making sure that generous little givers do not part with precious possessions, and many a beloved teddy bear destined for life in the Vatican has gone back home after receiving a pat from the papal hand.

At his first general audience instead of simply blessing a young baby held up to gaze at him Pope John Paul took the child in his arms, caressed his cheek and gently kissed him before returning him to his happy parents. Ever since, babies have been strategically placed in his way on every possible occasion, and family albums in homes all over the world now proudly display pictures of the great moment. The babies themselves seem to take these attentions quite contentedly, though now and then one protests. The Pope is an accomplished handler of these situations and generally manages to soothe away the tears and coax an answering smile.

His magnetic attraction for children knows no frontiers, and is far more than just a matter of imitation. A most affecting incident took place in Brazil when he was visiting the shanty-towns where people are too poor to have any means of knowing of being influenced by anything beyond their own straitened lives. As the Pope said goodbye to the ragged people and turned to leave, a little barefoot girl ran behind him and tugged at his sleeve. When he stopped and looked round the child held out

Above: *the Pope, in mitre and vestments after Palm Sunday Mass, collects a young admirer and escorts her to her parents.*
Right: *in the Philippines, the Pope left his elegant bamboo chair to welcome aboard the toddler who wanted a lift on his flower-decked carriage.*

Below: *high summer in St Peter's Square. Pope John Paul is all smiles at the serious baby trying his hand at a rather informal blessing.*
Right: *in the heart of Africa children came to him just as naturally.*

her arms to him with the greatest simplicity, and when he bent down, laid her head on his shoulder with touching confidence. The Pope was visibly moved.

To the set-piece occasions that fall to a pope's lot John Paul adds enjoyment and fun that his young listeners respond to eagerly. It has long been a tradition in Rome that as Christmas nears the children take their nativety crib figures to the Sunday Angelus for the Pope to bless them. The first time Pope John Paul was due to do this he let it be known he would like it if they all sang carols together. For more than the allotted half-hour he sang with them and conducted from his study window, and told the fifty thousand who had come for the ceremony that they must teach the old Pope, as he described himself, more carols so that they could sing them together at Christmas. Sure enough, on Christmas afternoon, quite unannounced, he appeared at his window and proceeded to lead the crowd in a rousing informal carol service.

A light-hearted man he loves to see children enjoying themselves and whenever he has the opportunity he joins in with a will. The gardens at Castelgandolfo, where he spends many weekends as well as the summer months, are nowadays regularly thrown open for the benefit of pilgrim groups and of the families who live in the district. Sometimes on his way to the swimming pool he comes across children playing in the grounds. His officials have long since ceased to be surprised when he stops to chat and joke, and have become quite resigned to seeing him take part for a few minutes in whatever games are going on.

Since he came to Rome he has been introduced to the local version of bowls, and tried his hand once or twice. Loyal shouts of "Good shot, Holy Father" greeted his first lucky throw and were duly reported with quite undue reverence in the press, which felt it tactful to omit to mention that all his following throws went very wide of the mark. The candid Pope must have laughed if he saw those deferential reports, because he himself had joked with the young players about his poor performance and wished them more talent than he seemed to be blessed with.

Though to children he is often a laughing friend and cheerful companion, Pope John Paul pays them the compliment of speaking to them very seriously, talking in simple terms of the happiness he is confident they will find in learning to know Christ and follow his way. He often stresses how much he relies on them: "you are my hope and the hope of the Church" is a phrase he returns to again and again. Many times he asks them to help him in his task through their prayers — and as his huge postbag from all over the world bears witness, very many children write to promise they will. It

is a service even a young child can render and thousands are proud to help their Pope.

He is deeply serious in his love and respect for children. The International Year of the Child, which began only three months after he came to the papacy, found him reminding the world that he could not be content just to regard with interest and sympathy the good initiatives that were to be taken that year. He linked the words of Christ "I was hungry and you gave me food, naked and you clothed me, sick and you visited me" directly to the helplessness of children and the moral duty to cherish and care for them.

When he urged the members of the United Nations general assembly to greater commitment to world peace, he asked them whether it could possibly be right that the children of the next generation should receive the arms race as a necessary part of their inheritance. It was a dramatic phrase, spoken with great intensity.

He is an impassioned defender of every child's right to life and an unwearying advocate of society's duty to make that life one of dignity in a peaceful world. His teaching against abortion and artificial contraception does not please those who take it as established that such control of population is a good thing in itself, or at least an inevitability in a crowded world. Pope John Paul will have none of this approach which leads, he believes, to a debasement of personal relationships and a distortion of fundamental values.

To many, and even to many Catholics, this seems a hard saying and too difficult for ordinary people to accept and follow. Yet it cannot be denied that the Pope himself who, in accepting his call to the priesthood accepted also the sacrifices of celibacy, is a powerful witness to the resources of love that are to found in a faithful Christian life. The world would be the poorer for the pattern of a devoted father if Pope John Paul, that most warm-hearted and affectionate of men, had not had the courage to choose as bravely as he did.

Above and right: *back home in Poland thousands of children came to be with the Pope at the sanctuary of Our Lady of Czestochowa and he was besieged as they ran to him with news of themselves and everything that had been happening since he went away.*

The Pope loves children dearly and children sense it and time and again, like this little girl, cuddle up to him with the greatest trust and affection.

A HORRIFIED WORLD

Early in the evening of Wednesday May 13th 1981 the news flashed from Rome that Pope John Paul had been gunned down in the very act of blessing his people and had been rushed to hospital in a state of collapse. It seemed that the appalling violence and terrorism of our times had claimed the ultimate victim, the man whose life of service was an inspiring force for good, whose radiant personality and passionate words of courage and hope for all men had given people everywhere a thrilling sense of the real possibilities of life. It was news to bring about near despair, yet it did more. The first reaction of anguish and sorrow turned to prayer, and out of the divisions and turbulence of our tormented age came an unforeseen unity.

Believers and half-believers of all faiths begged their God to spare the life now ebbing away. Others mourned and hoped for the survival of a fine and human leader whose secret they could not fathom but whose warmth and goodness they too had seen and admired. As reports came in that though gravely wounded the Pope might live, and that the assassin's bullets, fired at very close range, had providentially not penetrated any vital organs, there was a huge sense of relief, followed by fears that never again would he be able to resume the life that had captured the imagination of the world. Even today there are questions about how fully he is restored to health, and many questions that may never be answered about the events of that terrible day.

Pope John Paul was due to enter the great Piazza at five o'clock to preside at the regular general audience. Audiences had been retimed some months earlier when it became clear that the numbers wishing to attend were causing serious congestion as they streamed away at the height of the rush-hour. St Peter's Square on that day was not particularly crowded, though there were twenty thousand there. Among them were some hundreds of Polish pilgrims including a group from St Florian's Church in Cracow where the Pope had served as a young priest and where he is well remembered. Among other groups and parties was one made up of a hundred and fifty schoolchildren from Perugia. They were led by a Benedictine priest, Father Martino Siciliano, director of the observatory there.

He had been to many an audience in the past and was able to be of help to a young man on his own, a stranger to him, who was unsure where to stand. The young man approached the priest and asked him in English from which direction the Pope would be coming, Father Martino pointed to the Arch of the Bells and made a circling motion with his hand to explain how the Pope would enter the Piazza and drive all round through the barricaded aisles before the audience proper began. The young man thanked Father Martino courteously and walked away to choose a good position. Mehmet Ali Agca had taken the last step along the road he meant should

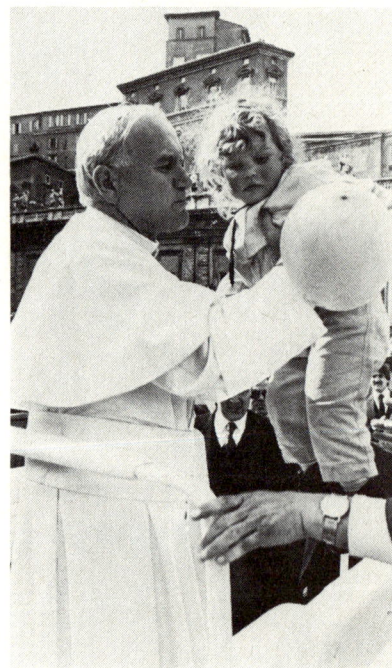

Above: *seconds before shots were fired Pope John Paul returns the little girl with the balloon who had been hoisted over the barrier to embrace him.*
Above right: *as the Pope turns to greet other pilgrims the man who meant to kill him raises his gun and takes aim (far left). The tourist who took this picture was unaware at the time that he was photographing a moment of history.*
Right: *the Pope falls back in agony. Another tourist taking pictures at the audience had his camera trained on the victim at the moment the bullets struck.*

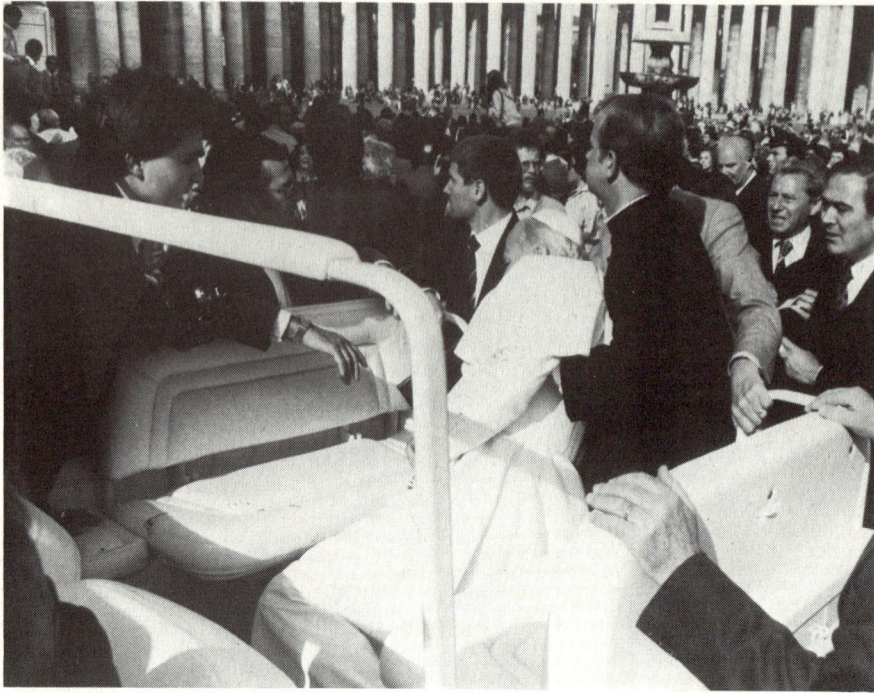

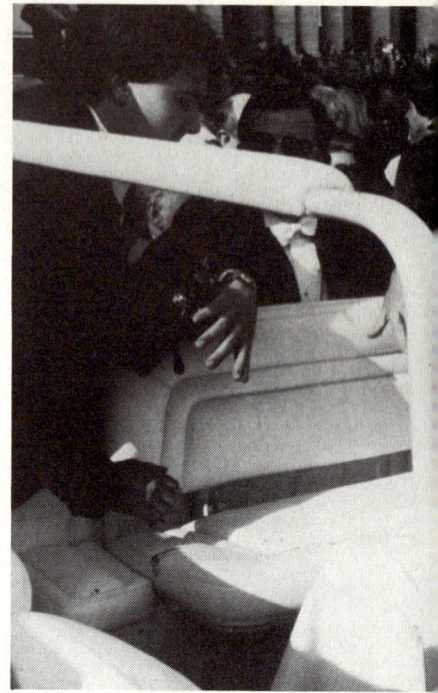

lead to the death of the man he saw as a vile and dangerous enemy, whom he had sworn to kill more than a year earlier.

A few minutes after the clock struck five Pope John Paul's white jeep drove into the Piazza, the Pope standing as always, and began its slow circular tour. In front, in his accustomed place next to the driver, was the Pope's personal attendant, Angelo Gugel, and seated behind Pope John Paul was his Polish secretary, Monsignor Stanislas Dziwisz. As ever, many of the tourists and pilgrims had brought their own cameras to take personal pictures of the eagerly awaited experience. The Press photographers too were out in force because, although a general audience is a regular weekly event, such is Pope John Paul's magnetism and informality that there are always touching and amusing little encounters to record.

As the Pope's jeep circled the Piazza, just as Father Martino had explained to the polite young enquirer, there was the usual flurry and hubbub all around him as people within touching distance stretched out their hands to him. The Pope smiled and stroked the hair of a dark haired child who called out to him and then, laughing, held out his arms to a little girl with blond curls who clutched a balloon and was being hoisted over the barricade by her parents to give the Holy Father an embrace. The child seemed worried. The Pope held her high in the air for a second or two, leaned forward to kiss her and then gave her back to the safety of her family. She was a sturdy child, quite a weight to lift, and as the Pope moved back to stand upright again he was momentarily unbalanced and had to shift position, which may have contributed to the saving of his life.

Instantaneously shots rang out. A flock of doves that had settled on the steps of St Peter's rose frightened into the air, distracting many eyes with their sudden movement. Pope John Paul fell in agony, collapsing into the arms of Stanislas Dziwisz, hit by four bullets at very close range. Four bullets had struck but two more had gone wide, one wounding an elderly American woman in the chest, the other fracturing the arm of a young Jamaican girl. As the Pope slumped back, a dark stain already spreading beneath the girdle to his white cassock and blood pouring from a finger of his left hand, Stanislas Dziwisz struggled to support him.

For a few paralysing seconds the Vatican security staff who walk behind the jeep and the people waving and cheering close by could not take in what had happened.

Left: *Stanislas Dziwisz rises to his feet to try to support Pope John Paul as he collapses, shot by the Turkish terrorist concealed in the crowd.*
Above: *security men come to the aid of the Pope to shield him from further attack.*
Right: *Franco Ghezzi (right) shouts instructions to other security men as Stanislas Dziwisz and Inspector Passanisi try to hold the Pope.*

98

Then Angelo Gugel scrambled across into the back to help hold up the ashen Pope, security men rushed up to form a living shield round the jeep, others dashed ahead to clear a path and, as the puzzled crowd watched, the driver accelerated and sped back across the Piazza and through the Arch of the Bells.

As the terrible realisation of what had happened began to spread through St Peter's Square a great sigh of lament was heard. Most stood motionless in bewilderment, still only half-comprehending the outrage that had taken place. Where the would be assassin., Mehmet Ali Agca, had stood a melee broke out as he threw down his gun and tried to shoulder through the menacing crowd. His attempt at flight seems only to have been a gesture. Overpowered by the police he made no resistance and was bundled into a police car and driven away, gazing impassively ahead as he shouted in a toneless voice that he didn't care about life, any life.

Many in the crowd thought that the Pope's injuries might be slight, and would be treated in the Vatican's own well equipped medical unit, but ten minutes later their hopes were dashed as an ambulance with siren blaring was driven out again through the Arch of the Bells and disappeared at high speed into the north-bound traffic. Evidently the Pope's condition was serious and he was being rushed to the Gemelli hospital.

As the news that the Pope had been shot reached the outside world television and radio in many countries interrupted their broadcasts and Vatican Radio's eye-witness account was followed with agonised attention. Messages of sympathy began to pour in expressing the distress and concern of world leaders. Her Majesty the Queen, in a telegram to the Secretary of State Cardinal Casaroli, said, "I was horrified and shocked to hear of the attack on the life of His Holiness. Prince Philip and I send our prayers for his recovery." Mrs Thatcher's message spoke of outrage. Archbishop Runcie, who had already begun to plan for the joint act of worship that will take place when Pope John Paul visits Canterbury Cathedral, earnestly begged all Christians throughout the world to pray for him.

Cardinal Hume heard the news flash on his car radio as he was driving to Gloucester Cathedral to speak at an ecumenical service. He said he was absolutely stunned and asked all Catholics to pray unceasingly for "the recovery of this dear man". President Reagan, who had been the target of an assassin's bullets only six

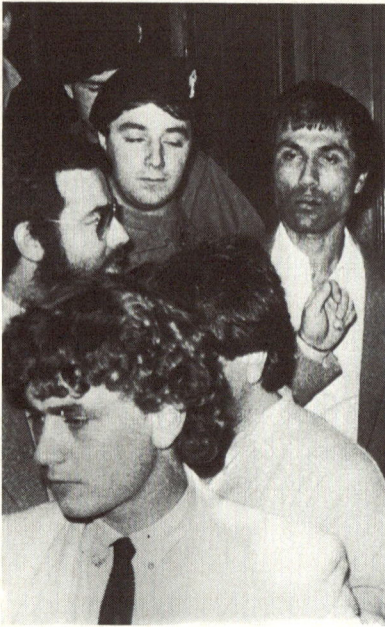

weeks earlier, made an immediate personal telephone call to the senior American Cardinal in New York to express the sorrow of all the people of the United States and to ask urgently for the latest information.

At the same time moving tributes came from men who lead nations of other faiths. The Prime Minister of Israel promised the prayers of all devout Jews for the health of the Pope. Egypt's President Sadat, who within five months was himself to die riddled with bullets and who had earlier invited the Pope to come and pray with him on Mount Sinai, condemned "a horrible crime against a man who symbolises the purity of Christendom – peace, love and brotherhood among men". The Turkish Head of State telegraphed to express his utmost sorrow, both personally and on behalf of the nation, and despairingly referred to the number of Turks who had been victims of terrorism. His distress was understandable because before the night was out it was known that the man who fired the gun was a Turk and he gloried in his act.

Mehmet Ali Agca remains something of a riddle to this day. From a modest background in south-east Turkey, where his widowed mother still lives with his brother and sister, Agca first trained to be a teacher at his provincial college, then went to Istanbul to study economics at the University. Whatever his views may have been earlier, within a few months of enrolling at the University he was deeply involved in violent extremist politics. The respected editor of the liberal newspaper *Milliyet*, which supported social reform, was shot dead in Istanbul in February 1979

and four months later the twenty-one year old Agca was arrested and charged with murder. At his trial before a military court Agca, who first admitted guilt and later denied it, giving as a reason his wish to cause confusion, claimed to represent a new form of terrorism and to have acted alone.

Condemned to death and awaiting execution, Agca made a mysterious breakout from a maximum security military prison disguised as a soldier, just three days before Pope John Paul was due to make his fraternal visit to Turkey in November of that year. Agca's first known act after his escape was to ring up the newsroom of *Milliyet*, whose editor he had been convicted of murdering, to tell them that he had left an important communication at their offices, and give directions where it was to be found. A hoax was suspected but the letter was discovered and contained Agca's statement that he would definitely kill the Pope if the intended visit to Istanbul was not cancelled.

The Pope was warned but was undeterred. He said, "I am not afraid. It is what you might call one of the risks of the job. We are all in God's hands and love is stronger than hate." He spoke with compassion about the "poor man, poor boy" who had threatened him. It is not known why Agca made no move against the Pope in Turkey. Perhaps the military guard was too strong, perhaps something went wrong with his plans. But evidently his hatred for the Pope was unrelenting.

His activities during the next eighteen months are still conjectural. He is thought

Far left: *Turkish terrorist Mehmet Ali Agca was seized by police within seconds of his attack. He had thrown down his gun and was attempting to flee but made no resistance.*
Below left: *police remove Agca from the fury of the crowd.*
Below: *a woman in tears is comforted by a nun as she weeps at the terrible event she has just witnessed.*

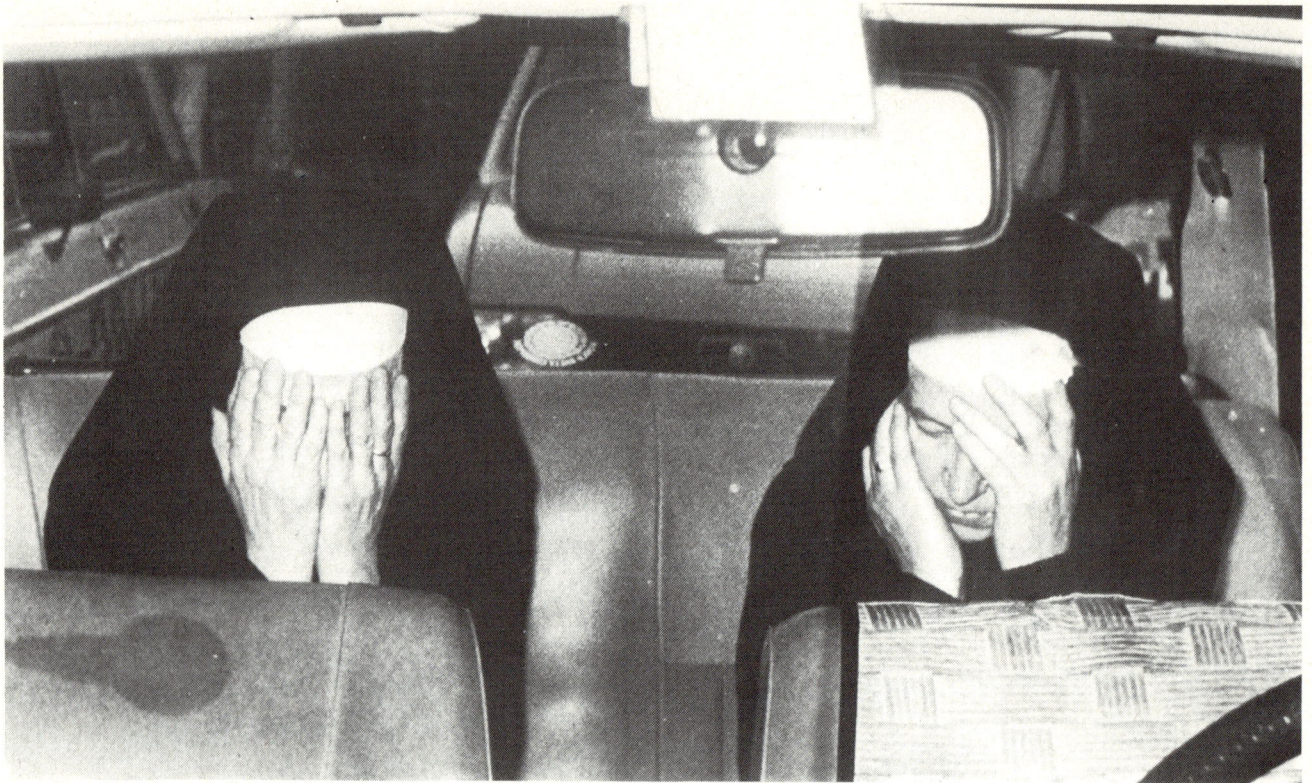

Above: *Polish nuns who serve in his household sat through the night outside the Gemelli hospital watching and praying that the Pope's life might be spared.*
Facing page, top right: *in unceasing prayer two women express the sorrow and intensity of the mourning crowd.*
Facing page, left: *deep in recollection at the second vigil in St Peter's Square, the anguish of millions is reflected on the face of this pilgrim, who holds a candle-decorated picture of the Pope for whom he prays.*
Right: *a candle's flame symbolising hope and intercession for the life of the Pope, lit by one of the thousands who kept vigil on the night of the assassination attempt while the Pope was undergoing complicated surgery.*

to have spent much time in Germany, where there are a million Turkish workers and it would have been simple for him to merge into the background. He later alleged that he had been in Spain, Bulgaria, Hungary, Iran, Tunisia and Switzerland. Undoubtedly he had ample funds for travel and several sets of false papers. In the spring of last year Turkish intelligence believed Agca might have gone to Italy and advised the Italian security authorities of a report that he had been seen in Milan. From there he may have visited Rome to make final plans.

In April he or an accomplice went to Perugia to enrol for a three month Italian course at the University for foreign students, but unaccountably never returned to the lodgings booked nor attended any of the classes paid for. Instead he went on holiday to Majorca and stayed at a well known hotel, flying back to Milan airport as one of a group of tourists on a Saturday night charter flight. On Monday May 11th he was already in Rome, booked into a small hotel, waiting his chance to kill.

After his arrest Agca claimed first to be a Chilean and then a Palestinian Arab. But a search of his hotel room brought these lies to an abrupt end. He had left a letter, evidently intended to be found after what he was convinced would be a successful attempt on the Pope's life. Written in Turkish it was boastful and quite without remorse. "I Agca killed the Pope so that the world may know of the thousands of victims of the imperialistic crimes of the Soviet Union and the United States."

Agca was quickly identified and made no attempt, when challenged with the proof of who he was, to deny anything. The only regret he ever expressed was when, on being transferred to prison, he shouted out to the watching pressmen that he was all right and was sorry about the two foreign tourists but not sorry about the Pope.

After some legal discussion about where he should be tried Agca was sent to the Rome Court of Assizes in July. He attended only the first day of the trial, when he disputed the right of an Italian court to hear the case on the grounds that he, a non-Italian, had carried out the act on the territory of another independent state, the Vatican. He made a long and lucid statement, addressing the court with complete self-composure. A distinguished writer present was impressed by his dominance of the proceedings and the intensity of his expressionless face and dark hypnotic eyes.

Agca then left the court and refused to take part in the trial. Despite his defence counsel's plea in mitigation, based on a supposed psychiatric disorder, Agca was sentenced to the full term of life imprisonment for the attempt on the Pope's life, the attempted murder of the two injured tourists and other associated crimes, with the first year to be one of solitary confinement. Whatever his future, his name will live for an act that brought universal grief. But he has one distinction many would be glad to share. Pope John Paul referred to him as a brother and without doubt remembers him in his prayers.

The prayers of millions and the devoted skill of his doctors helped save his life; as Cardinal Hume said next day when he preached at a special Mass for the Pope at Westminster Cathedral. No doubt all present as the Pope was struck down prayed for him from that instant, but public prayer began moments after the ambulance dashed through the Square.

A priest in the crowd mounted the steps of the dais, took the microphone and said: "The Holy Father has been wounded. Let us pray for him. Let us recite the Rosary together." A nun came forward with a beautifully framed copy of the honoured painting of Our Lady of Czestochowa and placed it in the Pope's empty chair. Below it Polish pilgrims heaped the scarlet and white bouquets they had brought to the audience. The prayers went on without ceasing, though many were too numb to join in audibly and everywhere in the Piazza desolate people stood apart weeping, and strangers embraced each other for a little human comfort.

Pope John Paul was praying too. After the terrible pain as shots tore through him and he groaned to Stanislas Dziwisz "I have been hurt", he whispered the prayers of the Rosary over and over again. He was still praying as the stretcher bearers carried

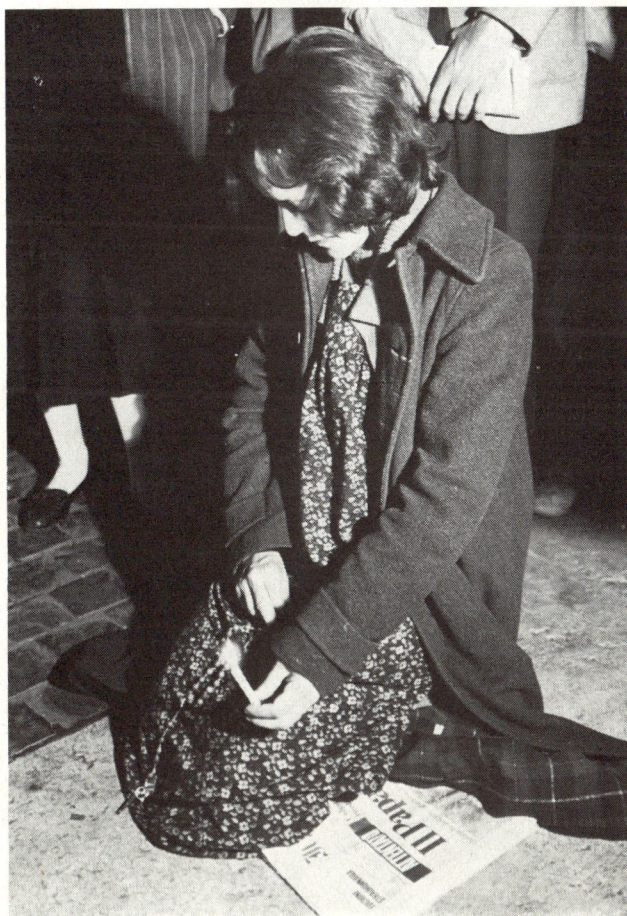

103

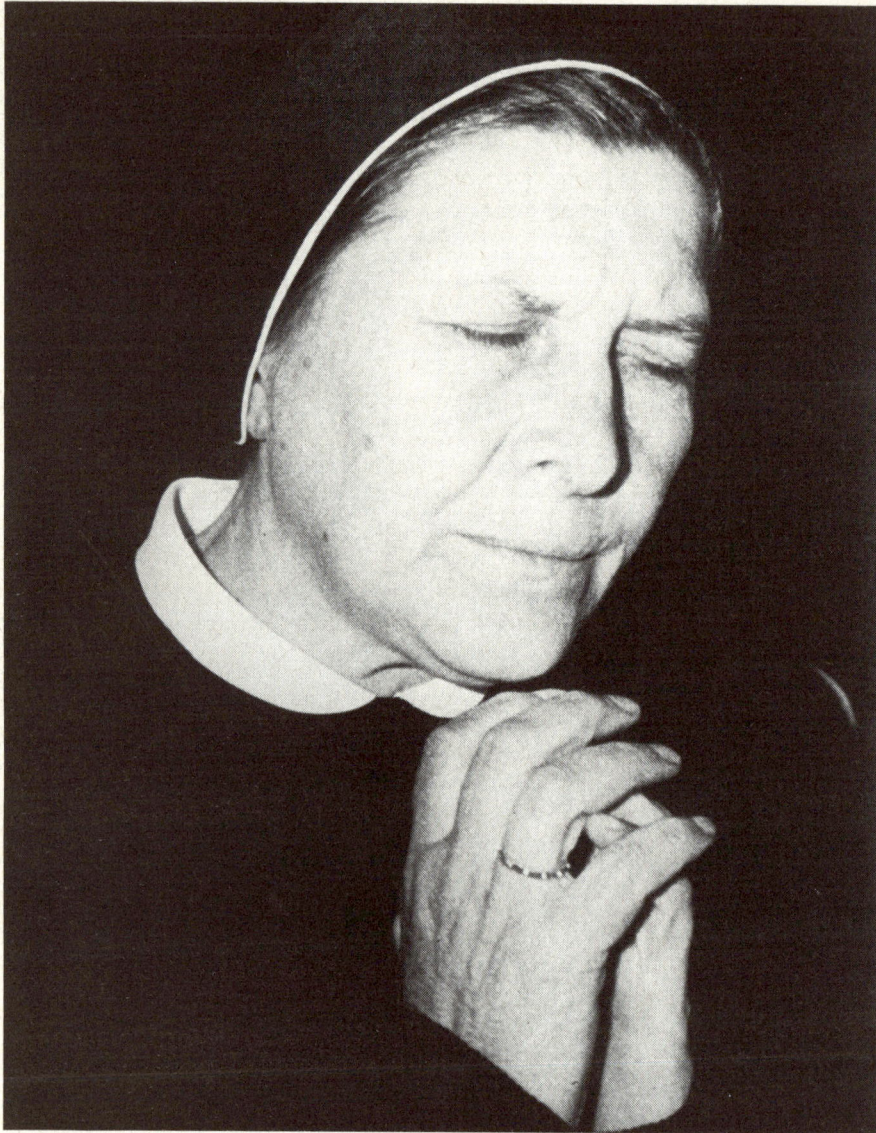

him into the Gemelli hospital, waxy pale, his voice almost too weak to be heard. He was still conscious, though, and able to make his confession to his devoted secretary and receive absolution. At five minutes to six when he was wheeled into the operating theatre, just over half an hour had elapsed.

Only minutes later the hospital's top surgeon, fifty year old Professor Francesco Crucitti, reached the operating theatre. He had been doing surgical rounds at another hospital on the far side of the city where he also acts as consultant when the first rumours came through. He telephoned to the Gemelli but getting no answer from the switchboard did not wait for confirmation but raced across Rome in his car, narrowly escaping a serious accident as he ignored road signs and swerved through no-entry streets, desperate to find some way, any way, through the rush-hour traffic.

Pope John Paul was already under anaesthetic, a tube inserted in his throat, and the surgical team were carrying out hasty checks. As Crucitti scrubbed up, they briefed him. Serious haemorrhaging was still continuing and the Pope's blood pressure was desperately low. After stemming the blood flow and giving him a virtually complete blood transfusion, Professor Crucitti was able to confirm that, contrary to all probability, no vital organs had been injured.

The news was passed at once to the Vatican and announced at twenty minutes to

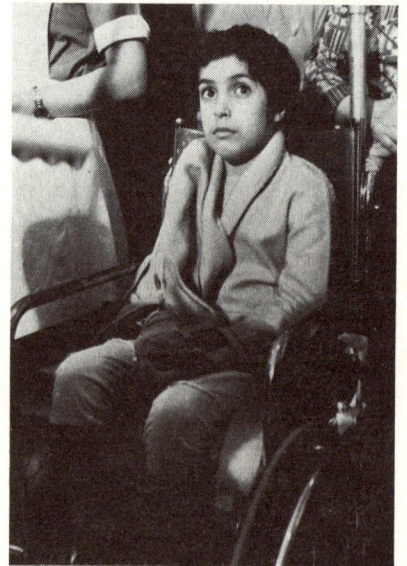

Above left: *that he may live is the petition of this sister praying with all her heart and soul for the life of the Pope.*

Left: *Marco Buongioanni, a nine year old fellow patient at the Gemelli hospital, wrote a touching birthday message to the Pope with his left hand, "the hand closest to my heart".*

Above: *thirty thousand people went to St Peter's Square to join in prayers for the Pope as he lay in intensive care. Public prayers began within minutes of the assassination attempt and continued until he was pronounced out of danger.*

seven to the tensely waiting crowds in the Piazza and then repeated in Spanish, French, German, Polish and English. A great cheer went up, but all were aware that the shots had been fired from only a few feet away and there must still be great danger to the Pope's life. The prayers continued.

The intricate operation to repair the serious intestinal injuries took almost five and a half hours. One bullet had torn through the abdomen perforating the lower colon and doing further damage as it ripped right through his body opening a further wound on his back. Another bullet had lodged deep in the intestines and had to be extricated with immense care. The Pope had also sustained injuries to his right arm, the left forefinger was broken in two places and there was heavy, painful bruising.

As the evening wore on the number of waiting people swelled as more came to St Peter's Square to keep vigil and join in the murmuring chorus of prayer. Shortly after eleven thirty it was announced that the Pope was out of the operating theatre and that the surgeons stated that technically the complicated surgery had been successfully completed. But the patient was running a high fever and for forty eight hours at least, as was normal in such severe cases, there must be great caution about his prospects for recovery. Thankful at least that the Pope still lived and that there could be hope, the waiting people sang Salve Regina, the great hymn to Our Lady that calls on her as the mother of mercy for her prayers in our sorrow and distress.

During the next two tense days, while the Pope remained on the danger list, in every Christian country special services of intercession were held and everywhere they were crowded. Preaching in Westminster Cathedral, Cardinal Basil Hume spoke of the attempted assassination as having made the Pope a living symbol of what the violence and hatred of this generation can do to the innocent. Now, he continued, the great teacher of peace had himself become the victim of violence. An American politician spoke of the Pope as the soul of the world.

Nowhere was there greater anguish than in Poland. In Cracow violent storms swept the city and the rolling of thunder and the battering gusts of rain almost drowned the voice of Cardinal Macharski, the Pope's successor as Archbishop there, as he repeated the phrase Pope John Paul had used so constantly during his triumphant return to Poland almost two years before: "We must be strong, we must be strong".

Each night thousands gathered in St Peter's Square to pray and watch for hours at a time, while others went singly and in groups to the hospital where the Pope was still fighting for life, to kneel on the pavements and in the car parks outside, reciting the Rosary and singing the Latin and Polish hymns they knew he loved and that they felt would give this brave man more heart and courage.

The world held its breath and waited for news as rumours flew round that the Pope was in great pain – sadly this proved to be true – that his fever was raging, and that his fatigue was disturbing. Though old friends, among them Mother Teresa of Calcutta, and senior cardinals went to the hospital begging for information, they were turned

Six days after the attempt on his life, his right arm in splints, his shattered left index finger heavily bandaged. Many were shocked to see how greatly the Pope seemed to have aged.

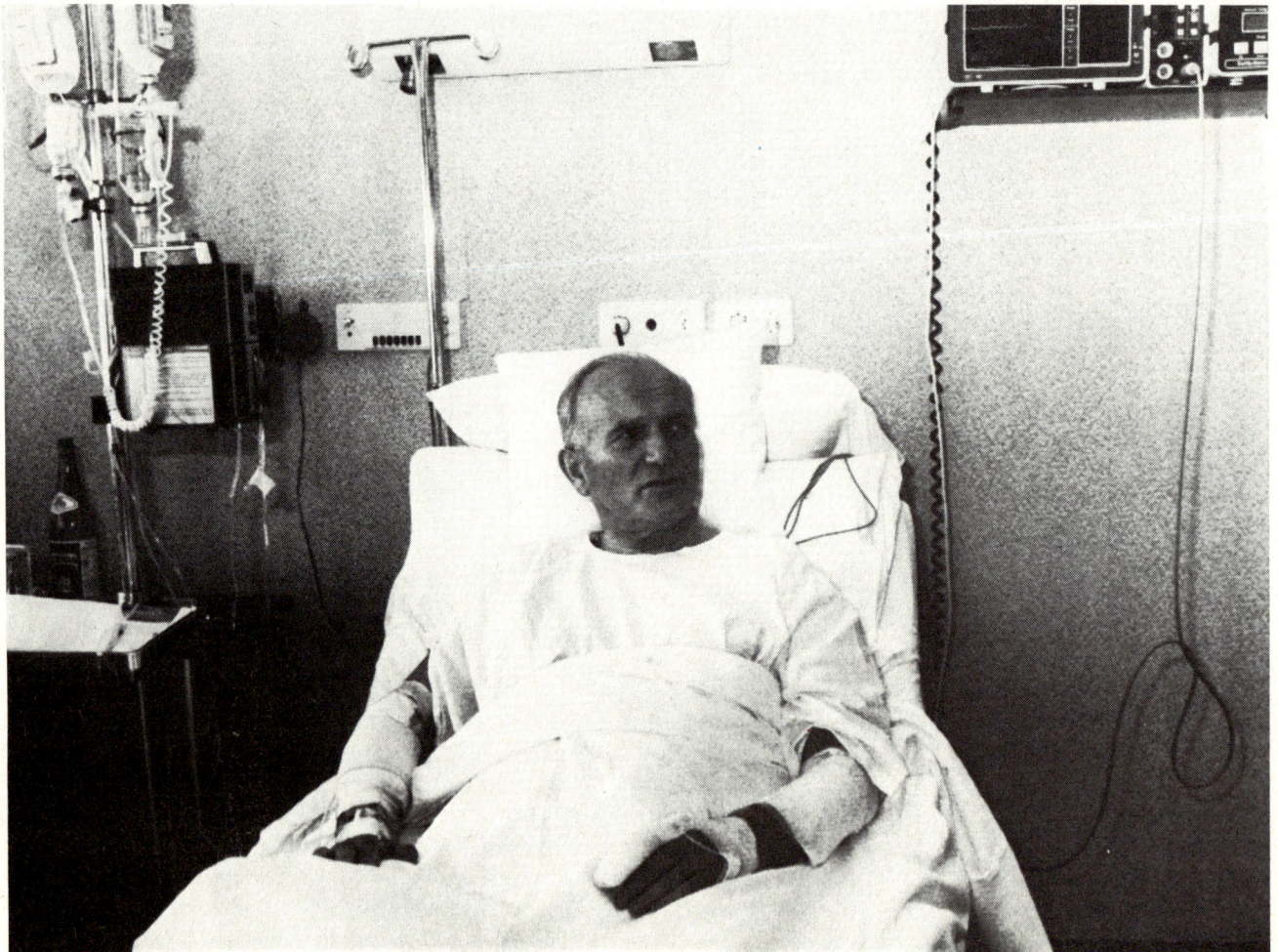

106

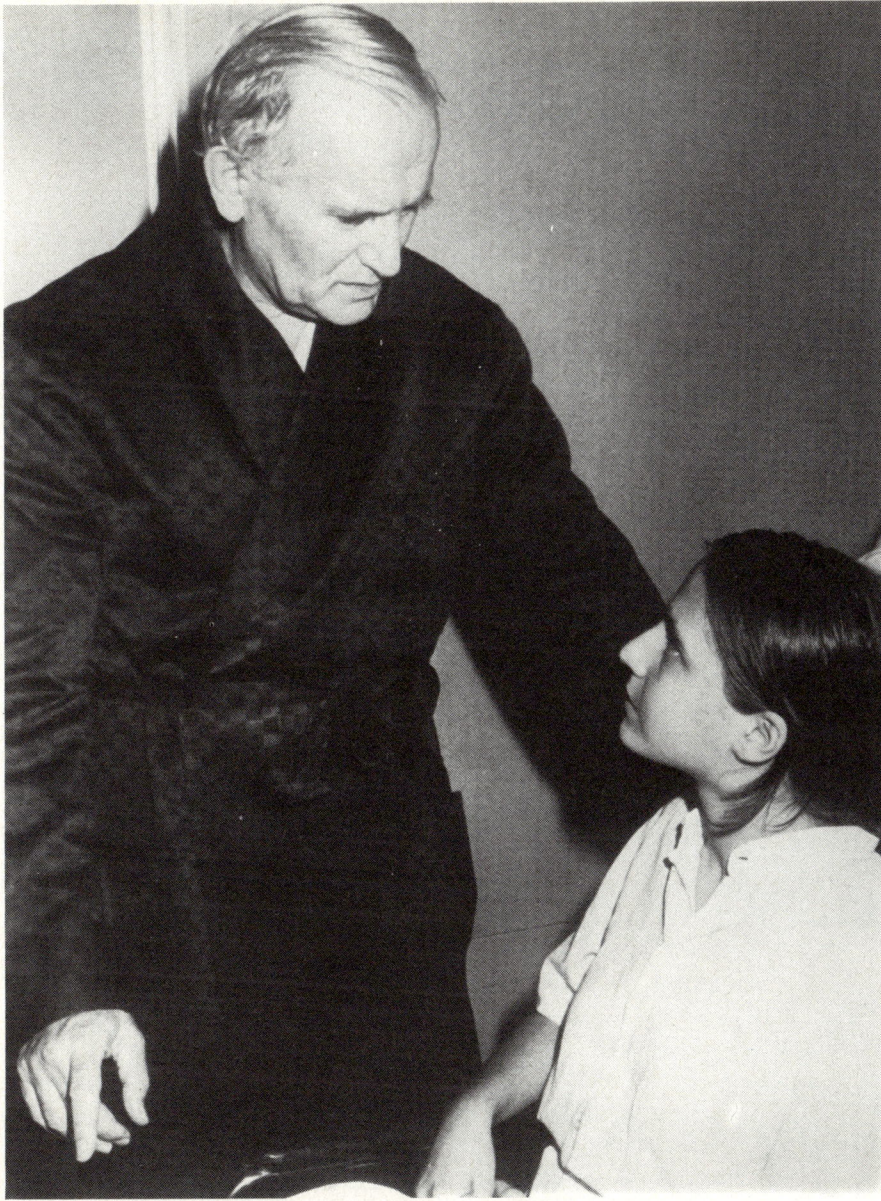

Wearing a royal blue dressing gown and on his way to a final medical check, the Pope stops to enquire after a girl admitted to the Gemelli after a road accident. As soon as he was allowed out of bed Pope Paul asked his doctors to let him visit fellow patients.

away and the doctors continued to issue non-committal bulletins. On the third day medical caution relaxed and reassuring words began to flow. The Pope's fitness and physical strength had come to his aid. His prospects were rapidly improving. He would soon be out of intensive care.

The Pope's first coherent words when he came round from the anaesthetic had been of forgiveness for the, to him, unknown assailant. The relief and jubilation was great when people realised that he was prospering so well that he was to be allowed to record a message to be broadcast at the Sunday Angelus. For the eighty thousand who flocked to listen it was a joy just to hear his voice again, weaker, a little tremulous, but vibrant with hope and courage, qualities he has made so much his own. It was the surest sign that he was embarked on the road to recovery.

He spoke more slowly than usual, but clearly, and many in the rapt throng wept at the familiar opening words of thankfulness and obedience: "Praised be Jesus Christ. Beloved brothers and sisters, I know that during these days and especially in this hour you are united with me. With deep emotion I thank you for your prayers and I bless you all. I am particularly close to the two persons wounded together with me;

Pope John Paul waves to wellwishers as he leaves hospital. Preparing to join him in the car is his personal attendant Angelo Gugel, who normally sits beside the driver.

I pray for that brother of ours who shot me and whom I have sincerely pardoned. United with Christ, priest and victim, I offer my sufferings for the Church and for the world."

In the days after his moving broadcast the messages and flowers and gifts sent to the Gemelli hospital redoubled. It was as if people felt it safe to take time from praying to write to him out of their affectionate concern. As he gained strength he was moved from the intensive care unit in time to celebrate his sixty-first birthday on Monday May 18th. In a tenth floor room with a distant view of the dome of St Peter's he was able to sit in a chair to read his cards and admire his presents. One short note touched him deeply. It had been written with great difficulty and in a very wobbly hand by a nine year old fellow patient at the Gemelli, Marco Buongioanni. Marco had attended Mass in the hospital chapel to join in prayers for Pope John Paul and afterwards wrote in a determined scrawl: "Dear Holy Father, We are all sad for you and praying hard that you will soon be well. I am a patient here too. I am sorry about my writing. I know it is bad but I have phlebitis in my right arm which is all strapped up. So at the moment I am having to manage with my left hand. But that is the hand closest to my heart. With love from Marco."

Pope John Paul's recovery seemed to proceed apace. The first pictures were permitted. Though the news of his health was getting better every day, people were shocked to see how much he appeared to have aged and how his features had sharpened as he lay in his hospital bed bandaged and wired up to monitoring equipment. He looked sombre and terribly strained, very different from the strong joyful man they had grown used to thinking of as the very pattern of a pope.

It was not only the pain. Pope John Paul was fretting. Feeling better, able once

108

again to say Mass, on which his life is centred, he longed for activity. Within days he was pleading to be allowed to do at least some work again. As soon as he was able to walk a few steps he asked to visit the other patients to share experiences of suffering together. When a few days later his last stitches were removed John Paul, gently defying medical advice, began to encourage his cardinals to bring their problems for discussion. A party of fifty two Italian schoolchildren who were to have attended an audience came instead to the Gemelli. Appalled, the doctors refused them permission to go in, and the disappointed Pope sent them a message of thanks for their gesture and expressed his wish that he could kiss each one of them for coming.

Clearly the doctors were fighting a losing battle against the indomitable Pope's will to resume his normal life. They managed to keep him in hospital for a few days more than they had feared, though not as long as they would have liked. There was further surgery to come, to reverse the colostomy that had been a temporary necessity until tissues had healed. But since his discharge was not totally against medical opinion, and since he so desired it, they let him return to the Vatican a few days before the great feast of Pentecost.

He was under orders to take things easy, and he tried to comply, but Pope John Paul's immensely hard working and self-disciplined life has made him a poor judge of what others would regard as taking more rest. To him life is accountable to be well spent in God's service and he has little concept of personal indulgence. He could not keep away from service and soon he was back in his stride. On Whit Sunday he made an unscheduled appearance within the Basilica of St. Peter's to join in the celebration

A word with Mrs Ann Odre from New York who was hit in the chest by one of the bullets intended for the Pope. In his first public statement after the shooting the Pope spoke of how close he felt to the two women who were wounded with him.

109

Mass. To the astonished eighty thousand who had not expected to see him he said simply, "I longed to be with you".

In the following days he fell ill again with fever and lung complications and on June 20th he was rushed back to the Gemelli with a serious relapse. As he fought his way back to health he was apologetic about the trouble he had caused and determined to submit himself entirely to his doctors' judgement. In fact he went further. Though they would have let him return to the Vatican, or if he preferred to Castelgandolfo, once his fever had abated, he knew himself too well to agree and decided to remain in their charge until his teatment was quite completed.

It was the beginning of August before the surgeons felt it was safe to perform the second operation, and a full week later before they willingly advised him that he might at last leave to convalesce. On August 14th, the eve of the feast of the Assumption of the Virgin, one of the most joyful feast days in the liturgical year, Pope John Paul returned home.

He passed most of his six weeks' convalescence at Castelgandolfo. Public engagements were banned but the doctors now knew that to forbid him to work would not aid his recovery. Professor Crucitti spoke of the Pope when forced to be inactive, or kept indoors and alone, as like a caged lion. Instead he advised his patient to spend as much time as possible in the open air and visitors were encouraged. A good ten years younger, in terms of physical fitness, than most men of his age, in his judgement the Pope would recover completely and get back all his energy and zest.

For people who went to see John Paul at this time, and were worried by the sudden fluctuations from apparent splendid health to great fatigue that they witnessed during the course of a few hours, the professor's opinion was very surprising. But Crucitti had come to know his patient very well and Pope John Paul has always had a talent for achieving the unexpected.

Above: *"I longed to be with you."* Pope John Paul explained his unscheduled appearance at Pentecost Mass in St Peter's Basilica a few days after his release from hospital.
Right: *welcome home. Soldiers of the Swiss Guard and the Vatican staff line the courtyard of St Damaso to celebrate the return of the Pope after all treatment was completed in August.*

110

THE MAN
OF GOODWILL

Immediately after John Paul had been elected Pope there was some speculation that, since he came from a country where the population was overwhelmingly Catholic and fervently religious, he could have little personal knowledge of people of other faiths and that, however sincere his commitment to Christian unity might be, it could hardly be grounded in experience. Like so many other hasty judgements this turned out to be quite wrong.

From boyhood he had made, and kept intimate friends outside his own faith. The Wojtylas, father and son, were on close terms with many Jewish neighbours in their small town, and known for their complete lack of prejudice. More than forty years later one of the first private audiences the new Pope gave was to the family of a school friend, a devout Jew who was by then the father of grown up children. The two men had been inseparable as boys in the same football team and had never lost touch.

Karol's personal contacts with Jewish friends had gone deep, and stood the test of the war years despite the danger. During the Nazi occupation Karol became a member of an underground group that helped Jews escape from the ghetto, found them safe shelter and provided new identity papers. After the war he was instrumental in setting up a society to be responsible for the care of the old Jewish cemetery in Cracow, where tragically there were too few Jews left alive to undertake the task.

As priest and bishop his wide reading and interest in ideas were never confined only to Catholic thought. Twenty years ago, speaking about prayer, he was calling attention to the spiritual values of Islam and Buddhism. Calling attention also to the personal demands of those creeds, the admirable courage of Moslems who pray at the appointed times regardless of where they may find themselves, and of the dignity of the profound concentration which Buddhists bring to their worship.

During his years in Cracow he was active in building bridges between his own diocese and the reformed churches. This was a particularly subtle and delicate task, as one Reformed Church bishop commented when referring with gratitude to the Pope's fine record of sensitivity in inter-church relations in a country where Catholics greatly outnumber Protestants.

He encouraged contemporary presentation of the Gospels. He was a very appreciative member of the audience when the young people in Cracow performed the rock musical *Jesus Christ Superstar,* and gave them permission to stage it in a church crypt. At his personal invitation the American evangelist Billy Graham preached in the students' church of St Anne to a congregation so packed that there was standing room only. It was the Cardinal's final inter-church initiative in Cracow,

The Pope has often expressed his admiration for the spiritual heritage of Islam and the courage of its believers in their faithfulness to prayer. In Africa he gladly embraces a Moslem leader.

In the magnificent setting of St George's Cathedral, Istanbul, the Patriarch of the West, Pope John Paul, and the Orthodox Patriarch Archbishop Dimitrius jointly conducted a service of prayer for unity attended by bishops of both communions.

and on the day he was unavoidably absent. He had been urgently summoned to Rome to take part in the conclave that was to elect him Pope.

He plainly proclaimed his commitment to Christian reunion on the day of his Inauguration. In his address he said he opened his heart "to all my brothers of the Christian churches and communities" and how much he valued their having wished to attend the ceremony. At the reception he gave for them afterwards he reiterated his firm resolve to go forward along the way to unity. In every country he has since visited Pope John Paul has sought out brother believers and made explicit his desire to draw closer.

His journey to Turkey had particular significance for Christian reunion. The Orthodox Churches, sundered from Rome for many centuries by quarrels that had much to do with tactlessness and misunderstandings, had gladly responded to the initiatives of Pope Paul VI. In 1965 a formal withdrawal of the condemnations of the past was carried out with solemn ceremonies in Rome and Constantinople. John Paul's fraternal visit to the Archbishop of Constantinople, the Patriarch of the East and leader, though not governor, of the Orthodox Churches, was an important advance. One of the Pope's titles is Patriarch of the West and by long tradition the Archbishop of Constantinople addresses him as "the eldest Brother". As a result of their meeting a joint dialogue committee was set up and held its first session on Patmos, the Greek island where St John wrote the Book of the Apocalypse, or Revelation.

Of St John it is recorded that when he grew too old to preach he would simply say to the people, "Love one another. That is the Lord's command, and if you keep it that

Above left: *Dr Donald Coggan, then Archbishop of Canterbury, with John Paul II at the reception after the Pope's Inauguration. Dr Coggan spoke of the Pope as a man of "warmth, strength and joy — the essential hallmarks of Christianity".*
Left: *the gold and silver cross, representing the mutual commitment to work for unity, presented in 1966 to Pope Paul VI by former Archbishop of Canterbury Michael Ramsey.*
Above: *joining hands with the Anglican Bishop Desmond Tutu, General Secretary of the South African Council of Churches, and Mrs Tutu at an audience in St Peter's Square. Pope John Paul has had wide contacts with the African churches since his days as Archbishop of Cracow.*

by itself is enough." Pope John Paul, who has said that he wishes his to be a ministry of love, expresses this intention vividly. At his meeting in Trinity College, Washington with more than five hundred representatives of non-Catholic Christian churches and communities he said: "It is a privilege to be able, in your presence and together with you, to give expression to the testimony of John that Jesus Christ is the Son of God, and to proclaim that there is one Mediator between God and men, Christ Jesus. In the united profession of the divinity of Jesus Christ we feel great love for each other and great love for humanity . . . the very desire for complete unity in faith is in itself a gift of the Holy Spirit, for which we offer humble praise to God."

Earlier in his visit to the United States he gave great pleasure to the Jewish community when he spoke to them about the common biblical heritage of Christians and Jews. He added poignant references to the suffering they had shared in his homeland.

Working to heal the wounds of the Reformation is very dear to the Pope's heart. He inherited an encouraging situation. In 1960 Archbishop of Canterbury Geoffrey Fisher took the initiative of paying a visit to Pope John XXIII and since that time, and the setting up of the Secretariat for Christian Unity under the late Cardinal Bea, a German, relations between the Church of Rome and the Anglican Church have become ever warmer. Many mutual misunderstandings have been thankfully set aside as the work of seeking the truth in charity, as Cardinal Bea loved to repeat, is carried on. In 1966 Archbishop Michael Ramsey presented a very beautiful cross to Pope Paul VI as a gesture of the increasing desire for full reconciliation.

Many problems were forecast before Pope John Paul visited Germany in 1980, for

Germany is the land of Luther, the central figure of the Reformation. The Pope spoke of Martin Luther as a witness of Christian living, and with gratitude of the present day generosity of the Evangelicals who had lent their churches to the minority Catholics of North Germany. He encouraged joint worship between all fellow Christians, Catholics included, saying "where we are gathered in the name of Jesus He is present in our midst." All of which should have come as no surprise at all to anyone who has studied the thought of Pope John Paul, permeated as it is by his trust in the integrity of the promises of Christ.

Pope John Paul is indeed a man of goodwill. There is no effort that could be asked of him to which he would not respond to make clear his total conviction that man finds his true dignity in the knowledge that he is the son of God, called to a high and eternal destiny of happiness. When he said at his Inauguration "with what veneration the apostle of Christ must utter this word: Man" he meant it with all his sincerity. He finds reasons for reverence in creeds which are far from Christian thought. In Japan he met Shinto and Buddhist leaders and told them, "You are heirs and custodians of time-honoured wisdom. We Christians are willing to collaborate with you on behalf of man's dignity."

During the days when the Pope's life lay in the balance people of all shades of belief and unbelief deluged the national press with letters expressing their personal distress and concern. A social worker from the north of England, who had had no contact with any church since childhood, voiced the thoughts of many: "I am not a Catholic, but the news of the assassination attempt on Pope John Paul II reduced me to tears. To me he symbolises peace and humanity – a leader who offers his beliefs to the world to be accepted or rejected. His respect for the beliefs of others is well known."

She had sensed, and responded to, something that is fundamental to the Pope's understanding of his mission, his generous goodwill and reverence for the right to follow conscience. Like everything about him these attitudes have deep roots in his immense respect for the dignity of the individual, and in the practice of a lifetime.

Below left: *with American evangelist Billy Graham whom he invited to preach at St Anne's Church, Cracow when he was Cardinal Archbishop. He couldn't be there because he was called to Rome to enter the conclave which elected him Pope.*
Below: *with Patriarch Tekle Haimanot, head of the Ethiopian Orthodox Church and leader of eleven million Orthodox Christians. This was the first meeting ever between an Ethiopian Patriarch and a Pope, a milestone on the road to unity.*
Right: *friendly relations with all branches of the Orthodox Church are warmly fostered by the Pope, here listening to the views of an Orthodox bishop in Germany.*
Below right: *Pope John Paul greets the Chief Rabbi of France, Rabbi Jacob Kaplan, during his visit to Paris.*

WELCOME TO BRITAIN

Pope John Paul was formally invited in August 1980 to pay a pastoral visit to the Catholic community in Britain. Cardinal Hume and Archbishop Derek Worlock of Liverpool were then at Castelgandolfo to present the report of the National Pastoral Congress, held in May of that year, when two thousand Catholic men and women from all walks of life and from parishes and organisations throughout England and Wales gathered in Liverpool to plan with their bishops how best to apply the Christian ideals in today's society. Delegates from other branches of the Christian church, the Anglican Bishop of Liverpool David Sheppard among them, worked with them on equal terms.

The thought that Pope John Paul might come to this country had in fact arisen immediately after his election. At the lively reception he gave for media people the day before his Inauguration he had shown himself very ready to go everywhere. Microphones were thrust in front of him by the international press who wanted to

Left: *Pope John Paul with Cardinal Hume in Rome. The Cardinal will be at Gatwick to welcome the Pope on Friday May 28th.*
Facing page, above: *Basil Hume, Cardinal Archbishop of Westminster with Sisters of Mercy in the Piazza of Westminster Cathedral. They will be among the nuns and religious brothers the Pope will address.*
Below: *Archbishop Derek Worlock of Liverpool accompanied Cardinal Hume to present the National Pastoral Congress Report and to invite the Pope to make his pastoral visit. The Archbishop has worked closely with the Pope over several years.*

know if this new and remarkably informal Pope meant to stay in Rome or go out to the people. Asked if he would visit America, Ireland, Poland, England the Pope had each time promptly replied that he would love to do so – if asked. At once invitations flowed in. By the time Cardinal Hume issued his there were so many other countries in the queue that he was surprised at Pope John Paul's ready agreement to come to us in 1982. Immediately on his return the Cardinal telephoned Her Majesty the Queen at Balmoral to tell her the good news.

The close inter-church relations cultivated in the past years by the Roman and Anglican churches had already borne fruit. The newly installed Archbishop of Canterbury, Dr Robert Runcie, had planned a visit to Africa where he was to inaugurate the new Anglican province of Burundi, Ruanda and Zaire. By happy coincidence Pope John Paul's first African visit, when he toured six countries, was scheduled to overlap. To the Archbishop's tentative suggestion that it might be valuable if Primate and Pope could meet there came a very warm response and a rendezvous was arranged at Accra for May 9th 1980, just three days after the National Pastoral Congress had been concluded.

The two leaders met at the early hour of seven in the morning and clearly the encounter went well. They quickly established a personal rapport and, impressed by the depth and spiritual quality, as he later said, of the Pope's listening, there and

Above: *Archbishop Michael Bowen of Southwark. In his cathedral, St George's, the Pope will administer the Sacrament of the Sick at a service on the afternoon of his arrival and preach from an outdoor podium.*
Right: *at Westminster Cathedral the Pope will concelebrate Mass with all the bishops of England and Wales, and administer the Sacrament of Baptism to a group of adults, before a congregation of six thousand. He will then visit the Piazza.*

Above left: *the Archbishop of Canterbury, Robert Runcie, invited the Pope, when they met in Africa, to make an ecumenical pilgrimage with him to England's greatest cathedral. Many Christian leaders from other traditions will take part in this important service symbolising a common faith. Afterwards they will meet the Pope for discussions.*

Left: *at the east end of the medieval cathedral of Canterbury is a new chapel dedicated to modern martyrs. Among those commemorated is Father Maximilian Kolbe, the martyr-priest of Auschwitz. As the final act of the Canterbury ceremony the Pope will lead fellow Christians to this chapel.*

Above: *Archbishop Bruno Heim, the Pope's official representative, outside the Nunciature in Wimbledon where Pope John Paul will stay while he is in the south of England. A heraldic expert, Archbishop Heim designed the papal coat of arms. His original painting is reproduced on page 2.*

then Archbishop Runcie made a most imaginative proposal. He asked the Pope, whenever he should come to this country, to join him in an ecumenical pilgrimage to his own cathedral of Canterbury. Without hesitation the Pope agreed saying, as he so often does, "I am ready". When formal planning for the visit began the invitation to the Canterbury pilgrimage was officially issued and acceptance confirmed.

Announcing that the Pope had agreed to make a pastoral visit to the Catholics of England and Wales – and to make a similar visit to Scotland which has its own Conference of Bishops, headed by Cardinal Gray who had issued a separate invitation – Cardinal Hume stressed the pastoral intention, the strengthening of religious life of Catholics in this country. The tone was to be, as he put it, frugal yet dignified. Any thought of pomp or ostentation would be quite out of place. By the end of the year the shape of the visit had been settled. Pope John Paul should be invited to spend time in each of the five provinces (the twenty-one Catholic dioceses are grouped together as the provinces of Westminster, Southwark, Liverpool, Birmingham and Cardiff) over a six day period, during which he would also travel to Scotland to be with the eight hundred thousand Catholics there. Throughout the visit there was to be special emphasis on the Sacraments, the signs of Christian life.

Proposals for the six-day programme went to the Vatican at the start of 1981. In May the shock of the attempt on the Pope's life put the journey to Britain in doubt. Great was the general relief felt when Cardinal Hume and Cardinal Gray went to see Pope John Paul in mid-October, just five months after he had come so close to death, and found him in excellent spirits and quite remarkably recovered, actively preparing, his enthusiasm quite unimpaired.

The plans submitted shortly after the Cardinals' return were considerably

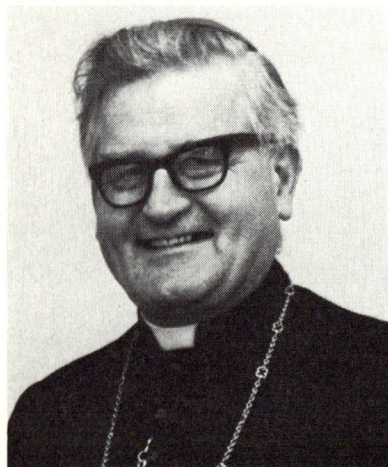

Left: *Cardinal Gordon Gray with whom the Pope will stay in Scotland.*
Below: *Bishop Francis Thomson is in charge of organising the Scottish visit.*
Centre: *Augustine Harris, Bishop of Middlesbrough. At Knavesmire the Pope is to preach on marriage and couples will publicly renew their vows.*
Foot of page: *Thomas Holland, Bishop of Salford is an old friend of the Pope's.*

modified because of the need to guard his health, allow for the extra security precautions all too plainly needed, and because the estimated costs were reaching alarming proportions. Virtually the only aspect of the arrangements not scaled down was the spiritual preparation. As well as individual preparations all parishes were to have a week of Mission during Lent. Every Thursday from Lent onwards is to include a special hour of prayer, ending on Thursday May 27th, the eve of the Pope's arrival, with an all night vigil. Many non-Catholics are pledged to take part.

From the beginning it was known that a meeting between the Pope and Her Majesty the Queen was, mutually, very much wanted. But delicate decisions were involved before it was announced that the meeting would take place at Buckingham Palace on Pope John Paul's first afternoon in England. At one time it had been thought that the ideal time to be received by Her Majesty would be after the historic Canterbury pilgrimage when Archbishop and Pope would together have led a service that formally witnessed the new charity between the churches.

This pilgrimage has been carefully planned over a long period and will include a joint reading of the Gospels, the reaffirmation of baptismal vows and the recitation of the Creed. In the congregation will be members of the General Synod of the Church of England, Catholic dignitaries and leaders of all the principal Christian denominations including the whole of the Free Church Federal Council, with the Moderator and other key Free Church leaders taking part in the liturgy.

The revised papal programme, though less arduous than that originally planned, is formidably crowded. But it should provide an opportunity for everyone who wishes to do so to go out and greet the Pope as his motorcade passes through the cities on his route. And the big outdoor events in the Midlands and the North are open to all-comers. Though tickets are necessary for the indoor ceremonies, many Catholic parishes have decided that non-Catholic friends should be given a share of the allocation.

It is taken for granted that at some time during the six days there will be a grand reunion between Pope John Paul and his fellow Poles living in Britain.

From Gatwick Airport on the morning of Friday May 28th Pope John Paul will go

Top of page: *Archbishop Thomas Winning of Glasgow, Scotland's largest diocese with nearly three hundred thousand Catholics. The open-air Mass at Bellahouston Park may be attended by a quarter of a million people.*
Above: *the Archbishop of Cardiff, John Murphy, has two big events scheduled for the Pope's final day. At Pontcanna Fields there will be a Mass for the people of Wales and the Pope will give First Holy Communion. The Youth Event at Ninian Park in the afternoon will bring together young people from all over England and Wales and is his last engagement.*
Facing page: *John Paul II, the Pope who loves to be with his people, as all of them hope to see him – happy, smiling, strong.*

straight to Westminster Cathedral to concelebrate Mass there with all the bishops of England and Wales before a congregation of six thousand, half of them outside watching on big screen television, and afterwards he will meet the people in the Piazza. In the afternoon he will be at the Palace to pay his respects to the Queen and other members of the royal family. Later he will drive across the river to St George's Cathedral in Southwark where he will be received by Archbishop Michael Bowen and will administer the Sacrament of the Sick, or anointing, at a special service for the handicapped and terminally ill, before preaching from a podium in the precinct. While he is in the south of England Pope John Paul will stay with his personal representative in this country, Archbishop Bruno Heim at the Pro-Nuncio's official residence in Wimbledon.

The next morning, Saturday, he sets off for Canterbury. It will be the first time that Pope John Paul has seen that magnificent cathedral and he will find there one chapel that will move him deeply. In the Chapel of the Twentieth Century Martyrs there is a memorial to his own great hero, Father Maximilian Kolbe, the Franciscan martyr-priest of Auschwitz. At the conclusion of the service he will lead a group of fellow Christians to pray in this chapel. Later on Saturday he will concelebrate Mass in Wembley Stadium for the Catholics of Westminster and Southwark provinces.

Much of his travelling will be by helicopter and that is how he will arrive at Coventry Airport on the morning of Whit Sunday to begin his five hour visit to the Midlands. Bishop Leo McCartie is in overall charge of what promises to be a spectacularly enjoyable occasion. Coventry Airport will be transformed into a great open-air cathedral and before the Pope's arrival there is to be a marvellously colourful pageant telling the story of Christianity in this country in drama, dance and song. At the Mass he is due to concelebrate with six hundred priests, including Cardinal Hume and the newly appointed Archbishop of Birmingham, Maurice Couve de Murville, Pope John Paul will administer the Sacrament of Confirmation.

On Whit Sunday afternoon he flies to Speke Airport on the outskirts of Liverpool. His old friend Archbishop Worlock, with whom he will stay overnight, has made sure that en route to the Cathedral of Christ the King the Pope will call at the Anglican Cathredal to meet Bishop David Sheppard.

Bank Holiday Monday will see the Pope in Manchester for an open-air Mass in Heaton Park where he will also ordain new priests. A former colleague will be there, Bishop Thomas Holland who worked with the Pope, then Karol Wojtyla, when they were both serving on Vatican Council commissions. A great welcome awaits him at Knavesmire Racecourse near York, where he is to address the people of the North East, including Yorkshire Catholics led by the Bishop of Middlesbrough, Augustine Harris, and a big contingent from the Newcastle area and couples will renew their marriage vows.

By tea time the Pope will be flying over the border to visit Scottish Catholics. Bishop Thomson has the mammoth task of organising arrangements and will be one of the party at Edinburgh's Turnhouse Airport. Here the Pope will be received by Cardinal Gordon Gray before going on to the famous Murrayfield ground where forty-two thousand young people will meet him in a Youth Pilgrimage. Later the Pope will travel by road into the heart of Edinburgh, to St. Mary's Cathedral.

The following morning, Tuesday, he goes by helicopter to Rosewell, to St Joseph's Hospital and on to say Mass at Bellahouston Park where as many as a quarter of a million will be able to attend the concelebration. The Archbisop of Glasgow, Thomas Winning will lead his brother bishops at the altar.

Pope John Paul's last day, Wednesday June 2nd, is given to Wales. The whole of the people of Wales will be represented at Pontcanna Fields, Cardiff at an open-air Mass in the morning, where Archbishop Murphy will receive him. The very last encounter of the first ever papal visit to Britain will be that afternoon when young people from all over England and Wales come to Ninian Park to pray with him, talk to him, listen to him – and give him a great send-off as he flies back to Rome.

We acknowledge with thanks the use of copyright
illustrations supplied by the following: Arturo
Mari. Associated Press. +BBH-Van Duren.
Camera Press. Colour Library International.
England Scene.
Epipress-Famiglia-Cristiana-Milano,
photographers Belluschi, Del Canale, Giuliani.
Felici. Interpress Warsaw. Keystone. Newspix.
Press Association. Rizzoli Press. Rusconi Press.
Universal Pictorial Press. Liam White.

Published by IPC Magazines Ltd., King's Reach
Tower, Stamford Street, London, SE1 9LS, at the
recommended price shown on the cover. Selling
price in Eire subject to VAT. Printed by or under
the control of Chapel River Press, Andover,
Hants., and bound at Redwood Burn Ltd.,
Melksham, Wiltshire. Sole agents for Australia
and New Zealand – Gordon and Gotch Ltd., South
Africa – Central News Agency Ltd.®

ISBN 85037 539 8.